UNEARTHED

The Lies We Carry &
The Truths They Bury

CHANCHAL GARG

First edition, 2025
ISBN: 979-8-9986875-0-1

Cover art by Brian DeSimone
Printed in the United States of America

A Personal Note on Privacy and Perspective:

This book reflects my personal experience and perspective. I don't claim to speak for anyone else, nor do I offer universal truths—only my own. Some names and identifying details have been changed to respect the privacy of those involved.

Praise for UNEARTHED:

Unearthed is a deeply personal, wise, and beautiful memoir of self-discovery and healing. Chanchal Garg illuminates the complexities of family, marriage, and cultural expectations, revealing how transformation begins when we dare to question our deepest conditioning. This luminous story will resonate with anyone navigating the delicate balance between honoring tradition and claiming their truth.

> — Kara Cutruzzula, author of *Do It for Yourself*,
> *Do It Today*, and *Do It (or Don't)*

A powerful, courageous, and vital read that dives deep into the reality of spiritual abuse, cult leaders, and what it takes to find your voice. In a world where many women of color have had their voices silenced, Chanchal arises as a powerful disrupter. A debut author to watch!

> —Jas Rawlinson, award-winning speaker,
> advocate, and best-selling author

I had a moment during a difficult time when a crucial insight emerged: *my power is not derivative.* As I read Chanchal's moving journey, I was struck by how many women never get the chance to come to this realization—despite it being true for all of us. Her story is both tender and fierce, and it moved me deeply. The way she names and reclaims her intrinsic power is not only personal—it's an invitation. More than just a story, Chanchal has written a critical offering for our moment—one that calls women back to themselves with honesty, courage, and hope.

> —Sheila Warren, CEO Project Liberty Institute

Unearthed is a searing memoir exploring how a smart, levelheaded woman falls under the spell of a so-called guru, tolerating sexual abuse. It accurately portrays how even loving families can damage their children, and the difficult road to healing. At times I wanted to shout at the protagonist yet always admired her honesty and courage in revealing herself. Chanchal Garg lays the story out in deft, beautiful writing. It will linger with me.

—Melissa Connelly, author of What was Lost, finalist for the Feathered Quill Award

Chanchal Garg traces her journey unraveling the beliefs that shaped her in this strong female memoir. As a trauma-informed executive coach and first-generation Filipino immigrant who's a proud daughter and granddaughter of farmers, I loved reading about how Garg approached breaking generational patterns, finding the courage to live on her own terms, and taking charge of her future—all profoundly feminist acts.

— Elaine Lou Cartas, Business & Executive Career Coach for WOC & Allies

Unearthed is a powerful exploration of spirituality, power, betrayal, and resilience. It will challenge the reader to reconsider the unquestioning reverence and trust we often give our spiritual leaders, while celebrating the transformative power of self-awareness, personal strength, and ultimately, freedom. This story will resonate deeply with anyone who has experienced abuse within systems of power, reminding me of the Catholic sexual abuse scandals. It will serve as a clarion call for survivors to break their silence and reclaim their truth. A must-read for those interested in stories of loyalty, lies and liberation.

—Rosie McMahan, author and counselor

In *Unearthed*, Chanchal offers the reader an opportunity to learn about her remarkable journey of healing from spiritual and sexual abuse. Written with remarkable candor and courage, she offers a window into the pain she endured as well as the hope she discovered in the power of connection, as she learned to show up with greater authenticity in service of more functional relationships. Today, Chanchal is one of our Leaders in Tech facilitators, embodying both the wisdom of someone who has traveled a most challenging journey, and the compassion of a leader committed to helping others heal. This book is a gift of vulnerability, strength, and transformation.

—Carole Robin, Ph.D., author of *Connect: Building Exceptional Relationships with Family, Friends and Colleagues*; co-founder Leaders in Tech; former Stanford Business School Director of the Arbuckle Leadership Fellows program

For Arjun and Sia,

You are the reason this book exists.
So many women in our lineage were never allowed to speak their truth—I want you to grow up knowing mine.
If life ever feels confusing or heavy, I hope you pause long enough to ask:
What is mine, and what have I inherited?

Know that your inner knowing is never wrong.
Trust your growth more than your mistakes.
Hold your dignity, even when you falter.
Be kind. Be bold. Stay true.

Your very existence made me look in the mirror—and because of you, I found the courage to become who I am.
I love you more than anything in the universe.
Even when I worry or stumble, know that my belief in you never wavers.

Always,
Mama

Dear Reader,

May you question the narratives that no longer serve you. May you find the courage to trace what you carry—and choose what to keep. And may you reclaim your truth, in all its beauty and power.

Contents

Author's Note

I was raised as if I were born in 1970s Punjab, India, even though my parents lived in New Orleans, Louisiana. Holding on to their roots was not just important to them—it was their compass. They immersed me in the rhythms of their culture, language, and faith, creating a bridge between a land I had never seen and the life I was living in the United States. They taught me values deeply rooted in tradition, while I navigated the contrasts between two worlds.

My paternal grandfather lived with us when I was born. Bauji, as we called him, was a tall, lean man with soft eyes and a slight hunchback. His movements were deliberate, each step slow and steady, as if he carried the weight of years spent in contemplation. Even though his gait sometimes faltered, his presence had a calm certainty, a quiet strength that spoke louder than words ever could.

My mother, standing just four feet, ten inches tall, is a fireball of energy and conviction. She always knows where she stands on any issue and is unafraid to speak her mind. For her, standing firm is less about defiance and more about balancing reverence for ancient traditions and elders with her own judgment. Service to others, particularly to elders, is woven into the fabric of her identity.

My father, slightly taller at five feet, four inches, holds his opinions just as strongly, but with a fear that his beliefs could be threatened or taken away. His emotional spectrum is vast: quick-tempered yet soft-hearted, capable of love and resentment in equal measure. You always know exactly where my father stands. There is no ambiguity—only raw, unfiltered emotion.

As immigrants, my parents fought to preserve the customs, language, religion, and traditions of their homeland. They did so with pride, even when it caused strain or hardship. It was as if each struggle reaffirmed their sense of righteousness, a belief that the sacrifices were necessary to keep their ancestral threads intact.

My story is just one among many. South Asian women, including those of Indian descent in the United States, are not a monolith. The vastness of India's traditions, languages, and customs is staggering; some sources claim there are more than 120 major languages and nearly 20,000 dialects. And as we immigrate, we each bring our own unique slice of that diversity, assimilating in ways that reflect both who we are and the new world we encounter.

In sharing my story, I recognize that my experiences, though extreme, are not universal. I know that my background, circumstances, and opportunities have shaped the way I see the world and the choices I've been able to make. I'm deeply aware that not everyone has the same chances or space to redefine their hardships, and I want to acknowledge that my path is not a blueprint for others.

If, in telling my story, I've unintentionally overlooked someone's reality, or if my experiences seem to suggest that the journey is the same for all, I ask for your understanding. My aim is not to project my circumstances onto others but to share the way I have navigated mine. My hope is that we can all see ourselves reflected in some part of the human experience, even when the details differ.

For those who, like me, have had the space to choose how to navigate their hardships, I offer this: reclaiming your power is not about following someone else's path—it's about finding your own. For many women, especially within South Asian communities, obedience, self-sacrifice, and silence are woven into our understanding of what it means to be good—good daughters, good wives, good mothers. Choosing to question those expectations, to trust your inner knowing, and to move in alignment with your truth is not just a personal act of healing—it can ripple outward, shifting generational narratives. This isn't easy work, but it's sacred work. And it's not just for ourselves—it's for those who came before us and those who come after.

Prologue

A name can weigh you down or set you free. Until recently, I felt the weight of names that others had placed on my soul as expectations of how I was to be.

When I was born, my parents asked my grandfather to name me.

"If her name (my mother) is Promila, then name her (me) Nirmala," he responded nonchalantly.

Though my mother intended to follow my grandfather's wishes, she associated "Nirmala" with someone she had little respect for. She shortened my name to Nirmal, meaning pure and unblemished—pure in heart, mind, intention, and action. Purity was important to her, and she often spoke to me about it.

"Your body is a temple," she would tell me when I was little. "Never let anyone touch it."

Why? People go in and out of temples all the time, I thought but didn't say.

My nickname was Nimi. While many thought it was a cute name, I never felt the significance of it. I did, however, feel the weight and expectation of protecting my own "purity."

My parents were very religious, and they introduced me to many swamis and gurus throughout my childhood. I was fourteen years old when my father first took me to meet Babaji, a leader followed by millions of Hindus around the world. He spoke a language from a region of India different from my family's. I couldn't understand when he spoke in his native tongue but desperately longed to learn. There was something captivating about him, and I felt a strong pull to connect more deeply with his teachings. A friend of my father's, a devoted follower of Babaji, noticed my eagerness and offered to teach me Babaji's language. This friend owned several hotels and suggested my father bring me to one of them for private lessons.

I should have been excited, but something felt wrong. The unease began the moment my father dropped me off at the hotel and lingered as I followed my father's friend into a quiet, dimly lit back room. It was set up like a family room, though it felt anything but familiar. He settled into a chair, his movements purposeful, and before I could react, he pulled me onto his lap.

A deep sense of dread settled over me, leaving me both disoriented and anxious.

I couldn't reconcile all that was happening. My mind was racing, but my body felt frozen, trapped in confusion.

I was fourteen, not three. I'm not sure I would have been comfortable sitting on his lap even at three.

He hugged and tickled me. I didn't move as he cajoled me to hug him back. Every once in a while, he was called to the front desk, and each time, I felt immense relief that he was gone.

When my father came to pick me up, I rushed him out the door. Once we were in the car, I asked him why he left me there for so long.

"I wanted to give you enough time to learn," my father replied.

Learn? Learn what? I wondered. "Well, he didn't teach me anything," I grumbled. I sank deeper into the front seat of the car.

My father looked at me. "What happened?"

What was I supposed to say? How do I explain to my father that I felt uncomfortable with this man tickling me? Would he understand? What if he made a scene and yelled at the man? What if he didn't? I felt trapped, not knowing what I wanted but knowing that what this man did felt awful. I longed for that to be enough to make my father understand.

"I didn't feel comfortable," I muttered.

"But what happened?" My father turned in his seat to face me.

How do I explain? I felt myself shrinking and wishing I were invisible.

"He made me sit on his lap and tickled me . . . and I didn't like it."

"Well, he didn't mean anything by that, *Beta,*" my father said, using a common Hindi term of endearment for a child. He seemed relieved as he started the car and tried to reason with me. "Maybe he was just being loving?"

"I didn't like it," I repeated, this time more boldly than the last.

As I said this, I wondered—Why couldn't I accept this man's affection? Was I wrong to feel uncomfortable?

But if my body is a temple, then why was it OK for this man to handle me this way?

I felt burdened by confusion and anger, both at the man and at myself. I felt a need to preserve my own purity, but I was lost as to how to do it, even though everyone around me made it seem as though it should be so obvious.

Part One

Buried Roots

"Identity is a negotiation between what is given and what is chosen."

— Bharati Mukherjee

1

Ramayana

The three of us sat on the floor before our altar in the basement of our home. I listened intently to the melodious sound of my father's voice as he sang the verses of the Ramayana. The maroon book with yellowing pages and rough edges lay in his lap, beckoning to me with stories of our ancestors and a sense of where I belonged.

I purposefully sat slightly behind my parents, drawing pictures on the beige carpet with my fingers. Avoiding my parents' eyes, I felt free to imagine the story on my own terms. The house was quiet, other than my father's voice, and the room was gently lit by the lights above the altar in the bedroom closet and the *jyot*, an oil lamp we had used for our prayers before my father began reading.

I tried to decipher occasional words from the readings and was delighted when I understood a line or two.

This book was the only inheritance my father desired when his mother passed away before I was born. I often thought of my grandmother and what it would have been like to read this book with her. As I listened to the stories, I sensed the presence of my ancestors and felt compelled to become a character in these myths myself.

Perhaps this embodiment would help me feel closer to my lineage and to my heritage.

"*Beta,*" my father said, switching from our native tongue to English. "Sita prayed to the Goddess for a good husband."

"Why did she do that?" I asked.

"Because a woman's place is always with her husband," my mother replied. She paused before continuing. "As a child, a girl belongs to her father, then when she gets married, she belongs to her husband, and then as she gets older, she belongs to her son. She is so precious that she always needs protection."

"Wow!" I paused as I tried to make sense of what I had just heard. "So, I'll always be protected?" I asked.

My parents looked back at me, pleased with my question as they nodded emphatically.

I didn't think to ask what I was being protected from. The pleasure they took in my question satisfied me. In that moment, I felt an unusual closeness to my parents. They were protecting me by sharing these teachings. I was grateful . . . for them, for the Ramayana, for my culture, and for the goddess to whom I could pray for a good husband.

Indian mythology is full of stories that aim to teach its people about the roles they must play to live a virtuous life. As an adult, my father told me that one of his goals in raising me was to ensure that I would not forget my roots. He and my mother read the *Ramayana* (an ancient Indian epic legend about King Rama and his exploits) to me daily as we sat in our *mandir* (temple) room. My father sang the lines in Sanskrit, and then they explained the meaning to me. After we discussed the story's lessons, I wrote a daily summary of what I understood in English to not only ensure comprehension but to practice my English grammar as well.

As a child, I didn't particularly enjoy having to write a daily report—especially on top of my sixth-grade homework—but I loved listening to my father read and hearing the stories that are so dear to my people. These stories helped me feel close to my family. A sense of belonging to a country that was thousands of miles across the ocean would well up in my chest. I heard the pride in my parent's voices as they told the stories of Rama's childhood and how he was a loyal son who developed discipline and a love for scripture and his gurus.

I absorbed their description of Sita—a woman who devoted her entire life to Rama, always placing his needs above her own. The one time she expressed a desire—for the golden deer—she was kidnapped by the demon king Ravana. From that point on, her honor was seen as compromised. It didn't matter that she had been taken against her will. In the world of the story, her proximity to another man was enough to stain her character. The implication was clear: once touched by someone else, even in captivity, she was no longer worthy of unquestioned belonging or protection.

Even after Rama rescued her, she was forced to walk through fire to prove her purity—and when she emerged untouched, it still wasn't enough. Years later, a village washerman cast doubt on her virtue, and that alone was enough for Rama to send her away. Pregnant and alone, she was banished to the forest, left to raise their twin sons without him.

As I internalized these stories over and over again, I knew who I was going to be. Sita's unwavering loyalty to Ram was undeniable— even if the men around her time refused to recognize it. My mother often reminded me to live in a way that left no room for others to question my actions. I took that to heart. I wasn't just determined to protect my purity—I was determined to avoid any situation that might invite doubt.

I am an Indian woman, I told myself. *And if I want to be loved and protected, I must uphold the values expected of one.*

I thought back to when I was three years old. We lived in a small home in Baton Rouge, Louisiana. I was standing on the linoleum floor of our kitchen as my mother rushed around, preparing for the day, when my father entered the room. I sensed a thick tension rising. They exchanged hurried, heated words that I couldn't understand. But I did feel the weight of their frustration and the unspoken resentment that filled the room. It left an indelible imprint on my young mind.

Though I didn't know what they were arguing about, I often heard them yell at each other, and I knew they struggled to get along. They were also experiencing significant financial hardship—my father had lost his job, and they were piecing together a living from miscellaneous work. Even at three years old, I could feel both their love for me and the burden my existence placed on them.

At that moment, my mother turned abruptly to my father and said bluntly, "Well, kill her, then!" While she never spoke my name, or even looked my way, I knew she was talking about me. I couldn't hear my father's response because I was too busy willing the ground to open and swallow me whole. When it didn't, I froze, unsure of what to do or say.

The shame and confusion I felt following this incident stayed with me for years. My parents were supposed to protect me. However, it seemed that I needed to figure out how to be and what to do to ensure that I was worthy of being safe.

Now, at age twelve, my thoughts began to wander outside the small family unit I had known, which consisted only of my parents and me. I began to crave the company of someone else, even though I didn't know who he was. I didn't realize how lonely I felt, but the thought of companionship thrilled me.

My mind swirled as I came back to the present and thought about the steps I needed to take.

"How do I pray for a good husband?" I asked.

"You can recite the same lines that Sita did to the goddess," my father replied.

"Karva Chauth is also a very auspicious day that comes in autumn each year. On this day, you can fast and pray for a good husband, and your prayers will be answered," my mother added.

I was so excited to get started. Getting married and having a person, *my* person, by my side sounded glorious. While deep down I longed to be seen, heard, and understood, all I knew was that there was something I wanted that I didn't have. The idea of someone who would protect me seemed like it might fill that void. I was too young to understand what "protection" meant in this context.

Someone who loves and cares about me, I thought.

It felt like pure heaven, and I could begin to pursue this goal now. From that year on, I fasted on Karva Chauth until I could see the moon. In the evenings before eating, I prayed for a good husband. I wasn't quite sure what would constitute a good husband, but I trusted that the Goddess would figure that part out for me.

***

Though I was born in Louisiana—a state in a nation my father had sought for the opportunity and lifestyle it provided—I often longed for more. I yearned for my motherland, to feel the dirt beneath my feet and to sleep under the stars on the clay rooftop of our family home in Punjab, listening to my father sing to me in the quiet night. Sometimes, I sat on the front porch of our house, closing my eyes tightly and picturing myself sitting in a mud hut in rural India, smelling the sweet scent of the earth, watching chapatis blow up like balloons over the homemade clay stove as cows bellowed for their young outside. I had countless visions of a life far more meaningful than the one I led, playing hopscotch on the driveway of our small-town home, sitting on the couch watching television, or watching my parents fight.

I wanted to experience true meaning, to live up to the ideals I'd been taught from the time of my birth. But often, I felt like the odd one out. The experiences I had—the things we did as a family—didn't seem to fit with my friends, even those who also shared my Indian heritage.

I thought back to the trip my parents had taken me on when I was just eight years old—a twenty-one-kilometer pilgrimage around Northern India's Govardhan mountain. For many kids, it would have been a huge struggle, but for me? It was completely magical.

Now, as I sat in my room, surrounded by posters of the actors and actresses who had played Rama and Krishna in the devotional television series in India, I remembered that journey. I could picture myself standing on the hot, gravel road, my bare feet scorched and aching as I followed in my father's steps. Just like my toes, the weather was blisteringly hot, and I was grateful for the spongey, darkening clouds that were beginning to hover and the cool breeze that washed across my sweat-stained face.

We were halfway around the mountain when my mother's footsteps fell into line with mine.

"Nimi, do you remember the story I told you about the mountain?" she'd asked.

"Tell me again."

"Well, when Krishna was a young boy, one day, Indra, the demigod of rain, got angry and began pouring rain down on the city," she explained. My smile grew as we continued around the mountain. "Even though Krishna was a child, he lifted Govardhan and held it up on his pinky finger as the citizens of the village and even the animals claimed refuge under it. The villagers were surprised, and many began to wonder who this little boy really was."

"Did they figure it out?" I asked.

"Not directly. This was one of many events that made the people around Krishna suspicious. Many believed he was God and treated him with this respect."

I'd heard this story many times over the years, and each time I loved it even more. For me, it was the inspiration behind this pilgrimage and the reason I wanted to complete the *parikrama* (walking around something sacred to pay reverence to it) of Govardhan.

The morning our journey began, I proudly took off my sandals and declared that I would walk barefoot as many of the pilgrims did. My father looked at me, puffed out his chest, and declared that he would do the same. My heart swelled with the pride I felt he had for me in that moment. At eight years old, I was embracing the culture of my father's homeland, just as he wished.

As we walked, I was stunned to see the various ways that pilgrims completed this trek. There were some who did it with pots of milk on their heads. There were others who prostrated their entire body with every step they took. I was humbled as I witnessed these levels of surrender and devotion. There were large and small temples almost every twenty feet along the path. We would stop at each one to offer our respects. At some temples, our guide would explain their significance. At others, I would simply bow automatically. Looking back, I'm not sure whether the devotion in my heart was obsession or love; at the time, it certainly felt like love. I often declared that the only true unconditional love was what we had for God, using this belief to justify my feelings and actions—even as friends and family expressed surprise at how deeply devoted I was to my religion and God at such a young age.

My feet became more and more sore as we walked barefoot on the gravel road. The final five kilometers were nothing short of grueling. I tried to hold on to my devotional thoughts and feelings as I felt myself longing for the end. I never admitted it, but I could not wait. After we completed this ritual, we were to drive about thirty kilometers to the temple dedicated to Radha Rani (Krishna's consort). When we arrived, I panicked to see the 225 steps leading up to this temple. I knew that I would not make it. My father spoke to the driver of our car, and they created a chair with their arms for me to rest on as they carried me up the stairs. I was grateful, but also concerned, since my father had also completed the *parikrama* barefoot. This extra effort, however, did not seem to faze him.

The rush of pride I felt, realizing I was contributing to something profoundly significant, was an intoxicating and unforgettable sensation. I soaked it up, wanting to stay in that feeling forever. Even as the years passed, I still thought often of that day. It had been a defining moment of my life—a moment where I was connected to my heritage, and therefore, to my parents.

***

My mother's connection to our homeland lived through her lineage.

"My father and his friends proudly guarded our village, both to keep us all safe and to make sure that our motherland was protected," my mother told me, describing the days following India's independence from British rule.

Listening to her talk about the ways in which my own family had been a part of India's revolution, I felt that familiar sense of pride. The strength and conviction my Nanaji (maternal grandfather) had felt was alive and well in my blood. At times, I imagined what it would be like to be a member of the Indian army, standing upright and at attention. In my childish fervor to defend my ancestral home, I envisioned fire shooting from my eyes and bolts of power surging through my veins. India was in no need of defense, but I was ready to stand for her just in case.

Unlike many of my second-generation Indian-American peers, who often resented the very things that set them apart, I held on to my Indian identity. For my parents and me, this felt like a quiet victory—especially in contrast to the other kids, who seemed eager to shed their Indianness in favor of fitting in. While they embraced their American identity wholeheartedly, I tried—unsuccessfully—to straddle both worlds.

I didn't want to simply blend in; I wanted to exist fully in both spaces—to feel a sense of belonging to a land far away while also feeling at home with my friends. But no matter how much I tried, the two cultures refused to coalesce. Instead, I found myself constantly negotiating—appeasing my parents' expectations while doing what I could to integrate into Western culture. The challenge, however, was that these two worlds didn't complement each other. Like mismatched puzzle pieces, they clashed, never quite fitting together. And with each passing day, I became more aware of that disconnect.

***

In the girls' bathroom, I reached into my school backpack and pulled out the small, black makeup pouch I'd carefully hidden. I gently picked up the square-shaped, mint green earrings my mother had told me I could not wear to school. I had paired them the night before with a blouse that had a hint of the same mint green in the floral pattern.

I cherished every moment of time before class in high school. I had been practicing winged eyeliner to create cat eyes, and I was hoping to showcase my new skills. There were a few other girls in the restroom, fixing their hair and chatting. I found an opening in front of the mirror and set my pouch on the counter. I put my earrings on and began to paint my face. The other girls all seemed to have their makeup on already, and some glanced at me side-eyed as I rushed to apply my own.

Once I was ready, I walked out of the bathroom, proud and feeling a sense of possibility in the air. The fire within me danced happily as I relished the freedom to choose and to express myself. I savored this time at school because it allowed me to escape the cage I was trapped in at home. Here, I could hold my Indianness in my heart while also being an American girl. I could explore my expression freely without worrying about my parents' disapproval.

The last bell rang, and a familiar churning started in my stomach. Joy, I'd learned, never got to linger. Guilt was quick on its heels, whispering that I'd done something wrong. Even in the thrill of my small daily rebellion, the bus ride home brought that old sinking feeling—like I was already in trouble. I reached up and gently touched the green, plastic squares hanging from my ears. How much longer could I keep them on? Until I stepped off the bus? Maybe just a little longer. I wished I could wear them forever.

By the time I walked through the front door of our home, the earrings were once again hidden in my backpack. In my mind, I was already humming the *chopais* (a quatrain hymn often found in Indian devotional poetry) that I knew my mother and I would be reading this evening.

At home, things weren't bad; they were just different. After school, I'd shower and then sit with my mother to read the Ramayana. She was teaching me Hindi, and I practiced by reading the poetic verses of this epic. I could tell when I had made a mistake in my reading because the rhythm and meter of each line would be off.

Each time I sat before this grand tome, its presence always pulled me in. The air felt fresh and pure, as if the space had been cleansed for something sacred. In my family, the Ramayana was more than a book—it was revered. The book occupied a place of honor on its own special altar, which had been lovingly crafted by my mother from a humble cardboard box. She had draped it in a rich red cloth, intricately embroidered with shimmering gold thread, transforming the ordinary into something sacred. The book rested there, commanding both honor and devotion.

I practiced singing verses from the Ramayana, and my reading grew smoother and more natural with each session. I experimented with different melodies, often losing myself in the rhythm and power of the resonating words. Those thirty minutes of reading together were a quiet ritual, leading us toward the final *aarti* (a devotional ritual of light offering), where we poured out our gratitude in prayer. Afterward, my mother would make fresh *puris* (fried bread) and potato *sabzi* (curry), filling the kitchen with the comforting aromas of home. I spread a stiff white tablecloth on the floor of our living room, and we sat down to eat, the atmosphere quiet and filled with the tenderness my mother had mixed into the meal.

Devotional practices reached into the depths of me—beyond soul searching, beyond words. I carried a quiet, persistent longing, like a low hum beneath the surface of everything. Most of the time, it felt like too much-something I had to tuck away or carry alone. But in prayer, in ritual, ache was allowed to breathe. Within devotion my yearning had a place to land. It didn't feel wrong or shameful there. Even when it wasn't enough—even when I still didn't know what I was reaching for—it was ok to be reaching. It was ok to be feeling.

I had always loved singing *kirtan* (spiritual chanting) and devotional songs, finding in them a space where my emotions could flow freely. As I learned to read the Ramayana, I became more recognized within the Indian community as a *kirtan* leader. Looking back, I realize my devotional longing often intertwined with my desire to belong—to be seen, loved, and respected.

My Indian friends would often joke about how boring *pujas* (religious rituals) were. When parents weren't in sight, they would mock the hymns and the sounds of Om.

"I like singing *kirtan* and reading the Ramayana," I would tell them.

They'd roll their eyes and walk away, whispering to each other.

I learned quickly that belonging required different behaviors and mindsets in different environments. This division inside me began to feel so natural that I didn't notice the exhaustion of code-switching multiple times a day.

Connecting always seemed to require a betrayal of some part of myself. When I followed my parents' rules and upheld their vision of a "good Indian girl," I felt like I was abandoning the part of me that longed for freedom. But when I leaned into friendships where religious rituals and cultural traditions were mocked, I felt like I was turning my back on my roots. No matter where I stood, a piece of me felt unseen.

I sat upright on the edge of my friend's bed, chest puffed out, hands stiff on my knees, fingertips forming perfect circles. The glow of her bedside lamp cast soft shadows on the walls, our open textbooks abandoned between us. It was early evening, and homework had long since given way to laughter as we mimicked the exaggerated behavior we'd seen in religious gatherings. Squeezing my eyes shut, I took in a dramatic breath and let out a deep, over-the-top "Om," sending my friend into another fit of giggles.

When I cracked one eye open, she was barely holding it together, her shoulders shaking with suppressed laughter. That was all it took. Within seconds, we collapsed onto the floor, gasping for air, tears streaming down our faces.

And yet, beneath the laughter, something heavier lingered. I felt the exhaustion of trying to be everything to everyone: the good Indian girl at home, and the normal (in the society we lived in) American girl at school. Two versions of myself that never seemed to align—like day and night, they seemed impossible to unite.

By now I was in junior high school and quickly discovered that my peers led completely different lives than I did. My friends spent weekends going to the mall or binging on movies and pizza at sleepovers, while my parents wanted me to focus on extra study, prayer, and chores. Mom and Dad worked hard to make sure that I was connected to my roots, and they did not seem to understand my need to integrate into American culture as well. I wanted to spend time with friends, experiment with makeup, and dress like the other girls—not to abandon my culture, but to explore who I was within it. To them, these things weren't just too American—they clashed with what they believed it meant to be a good Indian girl.

One evening, as my family and I sat on the floor with bowls of *dahl* (lentil soup) and roti (flatbread) spread before us, I felt a small pang of longing. I wondered what my girlfriends would be doing at that moment. *Probably watching the latest episode of* Beverly Hills

90210, I thought. Not that I knew too much about any of that. It was like another language to me.

Over dinner, I thought of my friend Rachel and the question she'd asked me during lunch. It was something so simple, yet I was afraid to voice it.

Turning to my father, I spoke gently. "Rachel invited me to a sleepover this weekend. Can I go?"

"What?" My father stopped eating, mid-spoonful. "Why would you want to do that?" he scoffed. "You're not *American*." He paused. "And anyway, we don't know these people!" my father added, his voice slightly elevated.

"I know them! Rachel is my friend!" I replied fervently.

"Friends," he retorted. There was a familiar, deepening scowl on his face. "You are not American. We don't just go to sleep at other people's houses!"

"Why can't I just spend time with a few of my friends?!" I asked, my resentment building despite the fact that my voice was getting softer.

"These influences are not good, Nimi. We don't know them!"

"Then how do you know that they are not good influences? You will never know them if you don't try. I'm not a robot that just does everything you say. I have my own thoughts and feelings!"

I ran to my room and slammed the door behind me. It felt good to express my anger in this way, but I knew there would be consequences to my behavior.

My mother's heavy steps came down the hallway, and the door to my room burst open.

"You think you can just slam the door like that? I'll teach you to get mad—you can stay in here!" She looked at me in that way that always inspired fear and then shut the door behind her.

Well, that's not so bad. I don't really want to go out there anyway, I mused.

I felt so relieved when I got to school the next day. The air at home had been thick with tension since my "defiant" moment, and I couldn't wait to see my friends. As I walked through the front doors of the school, I felt myself begin that familiar internal switch. Leaving Nimi outside and disappearing into . . . who? I didn't know, but I knew that Nimi could not come to junior high school with me.

Taking a deep breath, I ran through the halls to the place where my friends and I usually met before class.

Oh good, she's already here! I thought, smiling as I saw Rachel's face.

As I moved closer, however, I saw a change come over her. A dark cloud crossed over her usually sunny eyes.

"What's wrong?" I asked.

Picking up her backpack, Rachel moved slightly away from me, almost as if she were getting ready to leave. "I just don't understand you," she sneered.

"What do you mean?"

"I don't want to be friends with you anymore."

I stared at her—hurt and confused—as she looked at me with disgust. To my left, our friends stood by, silent.

I turned to them with a pleading look in my eyes. *What did I do? What did I do?*

No one said a word.

To my relief, the bell rang, ending the awkward moment. I was still wounded and wondered what I had done to upset Rachel so much.

When I got to our classroom, Rachel was already in her seat, looking down at her work. I walked up to her and paused.

"Rachel, I don't understand what I've done." I said, my voice trembling. "We've been such good friends. What happened?"

"Nothing happened. I just don't understand you, and I don't want to be friends anymore." Her face was as cold as stone.

Class was about to begin. I made my way to my seat, anger and sadness filling my chest. My face felt hot as I held back tears.

Why can't I be like the other kids? If my parents didn't want me to become Americanized, then why did they come here?

Sitting in the cold, plastic hollow of my chair, I bit my lip and tried to stop the tears that were threatening to spill out onto my cheeks. I felt like an alien, like the only one who had these two conflicting sides. And no matter how hard I tried or what I did to balance these sides of myself, I was never enough for anyone.

2

The Stage

"Now!" whispered the stagehand as she motioned for me to walk onto the stage during our high school talent show.

I took a few steps and bent down to touch my fingers to the ground and then to my head as an offering of respect and gratitude toward mother earth before I danced on her. I then took my place, posing in the starting position of my dance, in the center of the stage. The curtain opened, and I could feel every pair of eyes in that auditorium focused on me. I listened to silence for what felt like several minutes before the music began. My knees shook nervously as I tried to bring grace to my movements. *What if my knees buckle and I just collapse right here?*

A part of me longed for this collapse, which seemed easier than overcoming my nerves and beginning my dance. Somehow, I pushed that thought aside and focused instead on matching the beats of my ankle bells (*ghunghroo*) to the drumbeats of the music. After a few moments, my courage surpassed my anxiety, and I found myself lost in the movement and the sounds of my *ghunghroo* and music as the audience began to slip away. At the end of my performance, I brought my hands together in front of my heart and bowed in reverence to both the art and my own heart. I was startled by the applause that filled the room. Several people were standing, and I could hear my friends whooping and whistling in the crowd.

The stage, dance, and theater were my sanctuary during this period of my life. Strangely, I felt freer to express myself in front of people when I was performing than I did in real life. As I tried to keep up with the intricate dance of who I was at home versus who I was at school, the place where I truly found myself was on the stage.

Three times a week, I went to my dance teacher's home after school for my lesson in *Bharat Natyam*, a style of classical Indian dance. This art form was intense at times and gave me a workout I enjoyed, unlike the weekly treadmill sessions my father required. My dance teacher, Rangini Aunty, had transformed her basement into a dance studio with mirrors lining one wall. Though the room was plain, my experiences there were full of emotion and expression. Rangini Aunty sat on a rug on the floor at the front of the room with a small stick in her hand. I buckled the belt of bells around each ankle, and then Aunty began to beat the floor with her stick to create the rhythm. I stomped my feet so that my bells would chime in sync with her stick's strikes. It was as if we were telling an ancient story through beats, movement, and facial expressions. The hand positions (*mudras*) were very specific and, when used properly, became their own language. Through the movements of my body, the stomping of my feet, the precise gestures of my hands, and the facial expressions Aunty taught me, I transformed into each character in the stories my dances portrayed. I'd get lost in the stories until she stopped me.

"Not that way, Ma!" she called, using the Tamil word for those who are younger. "Bend your knees more and keep your arms straight. They are waving too much, Ma."

As I prepared for performances, I thought about how proud my father would be. I was embodying our culture. Many of the stories told in the dances were from the ancient epics of India, the same ones my parents had taught me to read and study.

One year, all my teacher's students performed the Ramayana. I so longed to be Sita, the wife of Ram and the epitome of womanhood. Instead, I was chosen to be Ravana, the evil king who kidnaps her and is killed by Ram in the end. I was devastated.

After the initial shock and disappointment, I settled into my role and even enjoyed it. The fight scene between Ravana and Ram was my favorite. The complex footwork, the ferocity required in my facial expressions . . . looking back, I can see why I was well suited for this role.

When the day of the performance came, I was disappointed by my father's lack of enthusiasm. Though he hadn't said it aloud, deep down I knew all along that he didn't like the idea of his daughter being on stage where men could watch her. I'm not sure how sexy I looked in that Ravana costume, but my father was not thrilled.

Despite Dad's disapproval of my being on stage, I loved my dance classes, and I loved performing even more. When I walked onto a stage, I entered the arena of my own imagination. I got lost in my performances. I could leave my own reality behind and immerse myself in the fantasy of the story I was portraying. I loved that I could barely see out into the audience due to the bright lights. It helped me feel free to revel in my own experiences.

My love for the stage further blossomed as I participated in choir and drama club in high school. The songs and choreography that we put to music made my whole being come alive. Each year, my school put on a play in the fall and a musical production in the spring, and each year, I would try out for both. The small parts I got made me think that despite my love for the arts, I wasn't very good at them.

Performing in the talent show my junior year, however, was a turning point. The week following this performance was filled with compliments about the dance, my endurance, and my costume. Each time I thanked someone for their kind words, I felt a surge of confidence rise in my belly.

Dancing *Bharat Natyam* on my high school stage took courage because I wasn't sure how something so foreign would be received. I longed to have bigger roles in the high school plays and musicals or to be a member of the school's show choir, Music in Motion. I wasn't sure if I could ever belong to these elite groups—or if they would even accept me. And if they did, I feared how my father might react. I watched the show choir perform every year, my body instinctively responding, as if I were meant to be up there with them. Auditions were a daunting challenge, demanding a solo performance as well as a memorized dance routine. The thought of it left me torn between exhilaration and panic. Though I had the chance to audition before my junior year, I couldn't summon the nerve to try.

By the end of eleventh grade, however, my longing overcame my fear. Preparing for show choir auditions, I thought through some of my favorite musicals: *Phantom of the Opera*, *Grease*, *Annie*, and others. I decided on one of my favorite songs from *The Sound of Music*: "Sixteen Going on Seventeen."

As I sat waiting my turn, I wondered if this whole experience was even worth it. *My father would be so mad if he found out!* And then, *I'm probably not going to get in, so he won't even know.*

I tried to put these worries aside so I could focus on my performance. *How many times do I get to be a senior in high school?*

I wanted my senior year to be special, and this was one way to ensure that it would be.

As I walked out onto the stage and motioned for the music to begin, I looked into the audience and saw Ms. Widick and Mr. Valley. Their smiles helped me relax. Mr. Valley was an incredible music teacher: always kind, fun, and so inspiring. Ms. Widick—our school counselor, theater and choir choreographer, and the mother of a wonderful friend—was also someone who put me at ease.

I began to sing, and after the first verse, my body loosened up. I glided across the stage, portraying the innocence the song suggested. *I was actually having fun!*

I sang the last note, and Mr. Valley and Ms. Widick smiled and clapped.

"Great Job!" Mr. Valley said.

I bowed. *Wow, I did it.* In that moment, it didn't even matter if I got in or not. I felt like I was walking on clouds.

Two days later, the audition results were posted on the school's office window. I waited behind a mob of people to see if I made the cut. When I finally got to the list and scanned it, I did a double take.

Wait, that's me?! I stared, looking for the word "alternate" next to my name.

I looked again. I was listed as a full-fledged member of Music in Motion.

"Nimi, you made it!" exclaimed my friend Andrea.

"I know, I can't believe it. I didn't think I would," I exhaled, pulling her in for a tight hug.

Just as I could feel a big burst of joy rising from within, the thought of my father's reaction descended like a black cloud.

I'll figure it out. There's no need to do anything yet. This is for next year. One step at a time.

I forced a smile as I attempted to protect that bubble of joy that had already started to fade.

Next year will be amazing. I'll make sure of it!

I didn't realize it then, but truly experiencing and holding on to joy was never something I had learned how to do. I had a pattern— every moment of happiness seemed to slip quickly into guilt or disappointment before I even had the chance to fully feel it. And no matter how much I wanted to, I didn't know how to make it stop.

***

I stood in front of my bathroom mirror.

Maybe a little more hairspray? I worried my hair would go flat as I danced the lead to *Dreamgirls* later that night.

I sprayed a little more just to be sure and dabbed a bit of lip gloss over my already deep red lips. After one more look in the mirror, I grabbed my heels from my room and ran downstairs. Approaching the kitchen, I peeked in from the doorway to make sure my dad wasn't around. My mother was cleaning up from dinner. I floated over to her, gave her a hug, and told her I'd see her there.

It was the night of the Music in Motion Gala at school. We had prepared for this night for weeks, practicing, organizing, marketing, and selling tickets. The cafeteria had been transformed into a ballroom with black, white, and gold balloon bridges, streamers, and sequined backdrops.

When I arrived, I could feel a buzz in the music-room-turned-dressing room. Members of the tech crew were busily going back and forth between Mr. Valley's office and backstage.

Suddenly, a pair of arms grabbed me from behind in a fierce hug.

Spinning around, I exclaimed, "Natalie—oh my gosh, you look amazing!" With her long, wavy hair pulled tight into a high ponytail and wearing our black, sequined show choir dress, she really did.

"You, too!" She grinned back.

I surveyed the room, and everyone looked amazing. It wasn't just the clothing and makeup; it was the joy on their faces. This was our night, and we were all so excited.

"Curtain!" a member of the tech crew shouted backstage.

It was time. We all took our spots on the dark stage behind the curtain as Mr. Valley opened the show with announcements and an emotional declaration of how proud he was of all of us. As we listened, we glanced at each other, smiling and relishing this moment of connection and contentment in the work we had done together. Finally, the curtain parted, and the lights came on. Along with the excited nervousness I felt, there was also a sense of community with the others on stage. My normal jitters were gone! We were performing for an audience, but it really did feel as if this was just for us. I glanced out into the audience as I performed and saw my mom a few rows back, right in the center of the auditorium. I smiled a little bigger. It always felt good to see her out there watching me.

Wait, is that Daddy? Oh. My. God.

It was. My father was sitting next to my mom, his face tight with tension, his brows furrowed deeply. Cold fury simmered in his eyes as his jaw clenched. I had to think about my next move rather than flow the way I normally did. Suddenly, I was terrified that I would forget the next step and botch the whole performance. My joy was gone once again, and in its place was that all-too-familiar guilt and terror over what was to come. I knew this wasn't going to end well, but the uncertainty of it all made my heart skip a few beats.

After that dance number, I sat backstage, knees shaking, and wondered what he was thinking. *Why did he come? Maybe Mom brought him? Why would she do that?* It distressed me to think about his reaction, but I had a whole show to perform, and there was nothing I could do about his presence now. *Maybe he'll be proud?* I shoved all my fear down as far as I could and forced a smile. Clinging to this very unrealistic hope became my life preserver—the only thing that would get me through the rest of the show.

Things were going as well as they could. And then . . . it was time for *Dreamgirls*. I had been placed front and center for this number, and as I lifted my eyes to the crowd, I could not avoid my father's stare. His eyes, once simmering, now blazed with a sharp intensity, slicing through me like a blade made of fire. His daughter wasn't just on stage—she was singing and dancing to the *Dreamgirls* theme song. At that moment, I wasn't sure if I would make it through the rest of the number. Though I kept moving, my legs started to tremble, and I was certain they were about to give out beneath me.

Finally, it was over, and once I was backstage, I made a beeline toward the chairs to sit down. I felt lightheaded, and my heart pounded in my chest. I took in a few deep breaths to try to settle my body. I was thankful for intermission and the chance to regain some composure before the second half of the show.

I dreaded the thought of the next few days at home. A heavy pit of anxiety was already forming in my stomach, but I shoved it aside.

Tonight, I was determined to make every moment count, to squeeze as much joy as possible out of the evening. The after-show gala was going to be so much fun—a chance to let loose and be with my Music in Motion family, the people who had become like a second home to me this year. I'd face Dad later, but tonight was mine.

After the show, I reluctantly followed the other performers as they piled into the lobby to meet their families. I watched as my friends were greeted with hugs, flowers, and exclamations of "Congratulations!" and "You were amazing up there!"

And then I saw my parents. I made my way over to them and hugged my mom. She looked at me with a tentative smile, her eyes reflecting uncertainty about whether or not to fully approve.

"What is this?" My father said flatly. A rhetorical question.

"What?" I asked.

"This is what you do at school?"

"This isn't school, it's show choir." I replied, trying to stay positive and keep a smile on my face. "Come on, let's go to the cafeteria. The decorations are *amazing*, and we're going to have a *Gala*!"

"You are not going *anywhere*, girl. I can't believe this. You are a disgrace to this family!"

I looked at him, my confusion and fear slowly turning to anger. "But this is our night, and I want to spend it with my friends! We've worked so hard for all of this. Please!"

"Friends," he said with a sinister chuckle, the word dripping with disgust. "You aren't staying here. This is a *disgrace,*" he spat, his eyes piercing into me with blistering intensity.

I fixed my gaze on him, determined not to yield in the silent battle of our stares. Even though I knew my night was over, I wasn't ready to surrender just yet.

A few of my friends came by and gave me a hug. "Come on!" they coaxed.

I turned away, my anger morphing into embarrassment. "I need to head home," I said in a soft voice. "But I'll see you at school."

They paused and looked at me. "Why?" they asked, glancing between my parents and me.

"My dad wants me to."

"We don't do this, and she is coming home!" my dad said to them in disgust.

They looked at me hesitantly. I could tell they weren't sure what to do, and the tension between all of us was too much for me.

"I'll see you at school on Monday," I said as I grabbed my mom's hand and began walking toward the door.

"Bye!" They waved and stood there watching my family and me walk out the door. I knew they were worried. I was grateful for their care and knew that I wouldn't be able to reassure them until the following week.

The drive home was silent. Once I got home, I retreated to my room and closed the door behind me.

I hate my life. I can't do anything I want to do. It's as if I'm supposed to be a robot that listens to every damn command that man has. He wants me to be Indian, and I am more Indian than any other child I know. It's still not enough! It will never be enough!

I reminisced about the recent trip to Toronto with my show choir, a journey that had been both thrilling and deeply meaningful. I had told my father it was a school field trip, and though he hesitated, he ultimately allowed me to go. The experience was unforgettable: we performed twice and enjoyed two captivating musicals.

I vividly remembered the night we arrived. I chose to wear a traditional *salwar kameez* to dinner—an outfit from India that included a flowing tunic and baggy pants. It was a symbol of my heritage, and I wore it with a mix of pride and nervousness. To my relief and delight, my friends embraced my cultural attire with warmth and respect, making me feel both valued and connected. Their acceptance made the trip even more special, allowing me to honor my roots while feeling deeply connected to the friends around me.

I was trying to blend and exist in two cultures, but I constantly felt as if I needed to choose between my friends and my parents. Later, I would realize that I had confused my loyalty to my parents as loyalty to my heritage.

***

Months passed, but my deep desire to dance and perform did not disappear. I continued to practice and perform as a member of Music in Motion while keeping it hidden from my father. During the week, he would stay in an apartment close to his work, about two hours away from home, and return to us only on weekends. This distance allowed me to keep my performing secret. I also became more vigilant about what I shared with my mother. I wasn't sure what she might tell my father, and I also did not want to put her in the difficult position of having to lie to him.

Spring had arrived, and auditions were opening for our school's musical. We would be staging a production of *West Side Story*, one of my favorite shows. I adored the songs, the characters, and the dance numbers from this play, and I was determined to land the role of Anita, one of the female leads. Anita was a sassy and intelligent Puerto Rican woman who spoke her mind and served as a confidante to Maria, the main female character. I loved the way she unapologetically told the truth and asserted herself when necessary. I longed to be able to show up this way in my own life.

A few days after auditions, the cast list was posted. I earnestly awaited my turn to read my fate. As I scanned the list, my heart dropped. I was not cast as any of the lead characters. I continued to scan and finally I saw my name. I was going to play the role of Rosalia, a supporting character. My mind raced; I was grateful to have been cast in a role that wasn't just the chorus, but I really wanted the freedom to fully express myself on stage as Anita.

Rehearsals began the following week. Each day, I entered the auditorium through the backstage entrance. There was a certain sense of belonging that anchored me every time I arrived this way. I loved being on stage even when there was no one in the audience and even when I wasn't performing.

A few weeks into rehearsals, I was sitting with Mr. Valley and Ms. Widick, talking about upcoming show choir performances. Suddenly, Ms. Widick looked at me strangely, as if she was holding back something she wanted to say.

"You know," she began—somewhat confidentially—"we actually wanted to give you the part of Anita."

I looked at her, confused, wondering if I had heard correctly.

Her eyebrows furrowed while the rest of her face softened. "We were worried about how your father might react, so we didn't."

Wait . . . I was meant to play Anita? I was good enough to play a lead role?

I wanted to go back in time. I wished I had known that they were worried about this so that I could have had an opportunity to make it right.

How could they not have told me?

I looked over at Mr. Valley, hoping that somehow he would make it all OK. He looked down and nodded his head.

"You would have made an incredible Anita. I really think you fit the part!"

As much as I was thrilled to know that they wanted me for the role, I was also devastated that I didn't get it for reasons beyond my control.

Decades later, this moment replays in my mind, over and over again. Even after more than three decades, I still feel it in my body: a sense of anger and disappointment at the many times I was denied such simple pleasures and opportunities, just because of my identity.

I was and am an Indian AND American girl. Yet, at every juncture, I seemed to have to choose, or someone else chose my identity for me.

I ached for more freedom—to make my own choices and to pursue the things I desired without fear of what my father or anyone else would think or do. Perhaps this is why, on days when there was no rehearsal, my friends and I would drive through Minnehaha Regional Park after school. It was an oasis of natural beauty sprawling across hundreds of acres of woods, meadows, and rivers all year round. It was spring. The bluish-violet flowers were in bloom, the greenery was lush, and the scenery was exquisite. As my friend Lena drove, I rolled down my window and sat on the frame to feel the wind on my face and blowing through my hair. On days when I felt something extra, I'd whoop and holler, knowing that only the trees and streams could hear me and wouldn't judge. Sometimes, we'd park and take the trail to my favorite place by the stream that ran through the park. In and around the water were giant boulders and moss. I loved to climb the boulders and run through the streams, feeling a kinship with life around me. The smell of rain and earth filled my lungs, and when I found a place that felt good—often on top of a boulder—I'd just sit and take it all in. It was a freedom that no one could take away from me, and I held on to that feeling until the very last moment, when the sky began to fade, signaling the day's end.

***

High school was a whirlwind of discovery, with each day feeling like a new chapter unfolding. As I walked through the crowded halls, I found myself searching for my place, trying to figure out where I truly belonged. Though I was raised to believe that boys weren't supposed to cross my mind until marriage, at sixteen I could no longer ignore the quiet pull of curiosity and attraction. In this way, I was just like many other girls my age, no matter our differences in culture, race, or religion. By the time spring rolled around during my junior year, what had once been a subtle awareness became impossible to ignore, rising with an intensity I hadn't expected.

About halfway through my third year of high school, my parents decided to spend a month in India, leaving me at home with my eighty-two-year-old grandfather, Bauji, who they trusted to look after me. I was thrilled, anticipating the freedom I knew was coming before they even left. Bauji rarely shared his thoughts, so I had no idea what he made of it all. All I cared about was that I had access to the car and the freedom to do whatever I wanted to do.

Each day, I'd leave home earlier than usual, thrilled that my mom wasn't hounding me about breakfast. Taking the wheel instead of a seat on the school bus was a thrilling taste of independence. I'd pick up my best friend, Lena, and we'd practically vibrate with giddiness as we drove to school.

About a week after my parents left, Lena and I were sitting in the school cafeteria together. I was halfway through my sandwich when, suddenly, I lost all awareness of my appetite. My eyes darted over toward the side door, my breath catching in my throat. Beside me, Lena put down her own sandwich and followed the direction of my gaze.

"Oh my God, *who is that?*"

"I don't know. Maybe he's new."

"Well, I know who's gonna get his number. *This girl.*" She winked.

I blushed as I tried to form a look of disgust on my face. This guy was gorgeous, tall, with a chiseled jawline, a slight tan, and beautiful hair that flopped to one side. I avoided looking at his ocean-blue eyes for fear that I'd melt into a puddle on the ground.

Jay, the German exchange student, seemed to command attention wherever he went. Every time I turned around, girls were huddled together, whispering and giggling about him, captivated by his presence. His sharp features and confident demeanor made him undeniably attractive, but I quickly dismissed any notion of him noticing me. After all, why would someone like him ever take an interest in someone like me?

With all the girls he has to choose from, I cannot fathom that he would even look my way, I thought, as Lena babbled on about who was going to be the first to ask him out. By the time I got home that day, I'd already forgotten about him.

The next day as we drove to school, Lena turned to me.

"So, don't you think the new German exchange student, Jay, is cute?" she asked with an expectant smile.

I looked at her, really confused. "What are you talking about?"

"The guy you were drooling over at lunch yesterday!"

"I wasn't drooling," I said, rolling my eyes as I tried to hide the slow burn in my cheeks.

"Uh-huh." Lena stared at me like I was missing something. "You know he likes you, right?"

"No way." I shook my head. "*Everyone* likes him. *Ella Hanson* likes him!"

She shrugged her shoulders. "Well, *he* likes *you*. He kept looking at you all day yesterday, and you didn't even notice."

Apparently, Jay had told Lena about his feelings for me a few days before, and she had withheld this information from me because she wanted him to tell me. I wasn't sure what this guy was attracted to, but I loved knowing that he was.

After this conversation, I started to put in a little extra effort as I thought of Jay while I got ready for school in the mornings. I looked in the mirror several times to see if I could find what he saw. I would never look like the popular girls at school. Their hair was perfect. Their jeans were perfect. Their clothes were perfect. Nothing too outrageous. Nothing too simple. Perfection. I was not that, and yet he still liked me!

I did not have the nerve to let Jay get close enough to talk to me. Every time I saw him at school, I made a quick escape. I wasn't sure how to be around him, so I decided that speaking to him on the phone would be much better. I told Lena to give him my number.

That night he called. The moment the phone rang, I knew immediately who it was.

"Hello?"

"Hi."

Silence.

"Ah, is this Nimi?"

"Yes . . . Hi."

"This is—" he started.

"Jay? Yeah, Lena told me." I interrupted.

"But how did you know it was me?" His voice sounded amused and curious at the same time.

"I recognized your voice."

"Oh . . . OK," he replied. I could hear his smile through the phone.

I don't remember exactly what we talked about, but the conversation was filled with short, awkward sentences. I felt braver speaking to him when I couldn't see his face, but my unease still lingered. I wasn't sure how to act or what to say. I lay on my stomach on my parents' bed, twirling the phone cord between my fingers and swinging my feet, trying to relax into the moment. Still, uncertainty clung to me as I stumbled through the conversation.

"Would you like to go to the beach party next week with me?" he asked.

Even though I had been hoping and waiting for this question, when it came, I froze. *What do I do now?*

"Hello?" His voice interrupted my thoughts.

I gathered myself just enough to respond. "Sure. That sounds fun."

He offered to pick me up, but I could just imagine Bauji's face if he saw a boy at the door asking for me. *Nooo, thank you.*

After I hung up, I immediately dialed Lena's number.

"He asked me!" I squealed.

"Yeah, girl! Look at you! You got a date!" *How did she always make things sound so normal?*

"You have to come with me!" I exclaimed.

"Uh, 'scuse me?"

"Dude! I can't do this by myself!" I pleaded.

"Ugggghhh . . . fiiiinne! You are *such* a dork!" She also had a way of making me feel oh-so-loved.

On the day of the party, Lena came over so we could get ready together. As we got dressed, we playfully pretended to be professional hairdressers and makeup artists, styling each other with exaggerated flair. Big hair and statement earrings were all the rage in the early 90s, so we teased each other's hair sky-high and chose long, dangling earrings to complete our looks. After making a few final adjustments, we stepped back to admire our reflection in the mirror with a quiet sense of joy. With a shared nod of approval, we hopped into the car and headed off to school.

As we approached the school parking lot, my legs grew progressively heavier until they felt like tree trunks rooted to the floormat.

"Leen, I don't know if I can do this!" I whispered, looking at her and feeling terrified.

"Dude, you got this." She smiled, urging me toward the door. "And I'm right here."

Lena always had my back. She encouraged me to believe in myself and supported me when I was too scared to take a leap. I let out a huge sigh and walked in behind her.

She stopped abruptly. "There he is!"

I followed her gaze and found Jay. *Crap*, I thought. My entire body felt like Jell-O.

Lena walked toward my date, and I had no choice but to follow, like a helpless blob dragging itself along the floor.

"Hi!" Lena said.

"Hi," he said, cocking his head to look behind her at me.

I awkwardly raised my hand for a tiny wave. He smiled warmly.

"Well, I'll just leave you two to it!" Lena said, looking from Jay to me. And with that, she walked away.

WTF. Where is she going? I can't do this on my own, I thought nervously.

With Lena off in the distance, I turned—even more awkwardly—toward Jay and tried to make up for the way I was feeling inside. But the words just wouldn't come out. I was grateful when he offered to get us something to drink and then led me to a couple of empty seats on a bench. For a while, we sat and talked . . . . Well, he spoke, and I listened. As each minute passed, my anxiety grew, and soon, I was barely able to keep up with what he was saying.

I was stuck in my head when I suddenly felt his hand gently wrap around mine. Startled, I pulled quickly away, then stared at my hand and immediately regretted my reaction. I had no idea how to handle the moment. Secretly, I wanted to hold his hand, but my nerves had taken over. Suddenly, I felt hands on my back, and before I knew it, I was shoved forward onto my feet. Jay stumbled forward too, caught off guard. Spinning around, we found Lena standing there, grinning proudly, thrilled with her not-so-subtle attempt to get us talking more.

I locked eyes with her, silently willing her to understand what I was thinking. When she didn't seem to get it, I quickly and abruptly walked by her, expecting her to follow me.

"I need to talk to you," I hissed under my breath as I headed straight for the girl's bathroom.

Once inside, my body softened, and I turned around to face her.

"I can't do this," I exhaled, feeling an unexpected wave of emotion as tears welled up in my eyes. "We have to leave."

Lena stared at me, waiting to see if I had finished. "*Now!*"

"What?" she replied, realizing I was serious. "We just got here!"

"I know, but I need to go home . . . I can't do this!"

"OK, OK," she said. "What do you want me to tell him?"

I looked down. "I don't know."

Drowning in an ocean of shame and embarrassment, I snuck out of the bathroom and headed for the side door to the parking lot. I made sure Jay wouldn't see me leaving.

Lena went to talk to Jay and later shared the conversation with me.

"What's wrong with your friend?" he asked. "I'm trying to talk to her, but she doesn't talk."

"No—she's not like that. You just have to get to know her, that's all," Lena replied.

"Well, I'm trying, but it's so awkward! I don't think I'm comfortable being with her," he said apologetically.

I pictured Lena raising her voice—her chin following suit. "Well, she isn't comfortable with you, either." And with that, she spun around and joined me in the parking lot.

"What did he say?" I asked her timidly.

She told me everything. Lena wasn't one to withhold the truth.

"Ugh. He hates me!" I exclaimed. "I don't know what's wrong with me . . . I just couldn't talk to him!"

"Dude, don't worry about it—it's fine. He's a little weird anyway." She chuckled.

I was so grateful for Lena and her ability to keep things light. I let out a huge sigh and glanced ruefully at my friend.

She gave me a look that reiterated all the support she had offered me that evening. I don't know what I would have done without her. This was my first experience of any sort of "date," and although it was a complete disaster, I didn't have to do it alone, thanks to Lena.

3

Devotion

When I was twelve, my father took me to yet another *kirtan* gathering—something we did often. This time, we were visiting my uncle in Baton Rouge, Louisiana, and he couldn't stop raving about a woman from India who was in town. He spoke of her voice—rich, soulful, and filled with devotion—as if it carried something sacred within it.

We arrived to find a mansion towering before us. The grand front door stood wide open, welcoming everyone inside. Polished marble floors gleamed, and, just ahead, a staircase wound elegantly toward the upper floors. We slipped off our shoes and walked past walls lined with expensive art. Drawn by the sound of singing voices, we followed the melody through the house toward the main living area.

A woman dressed in an orange cotton sari sat on a makeshift stage. She was playing the harmonium (a small hand-pumped keyboard instrument popular in Indian devotional music), and a man sat slightly behind her, keeping the beat with *tablas* (a pair of hand-played Indian drums). I sat on the floor, which was covered with white sheets, and listened to the woman on stage, singing to Lord

Krishna. Her voice was rich and carried a deep sense of love and yearning that resonated with every note. The tears running down her face drew me in. I could feel her devotion, and my own eyes welled up with tears as I listened. This woman and her voice were magical. She seemed to have a relationship with the divine. I wanted that. As I listened, I felt an irresistible urge to learn from her.

After the event, my father and other attendees sat and chatted with her as they drank chai. I settled on the floor next to my father and listened. The singer, *"Didi"* ("big sister" as they called her), spoke of her guru back in India and how she and many others had become close to God through him. Her charisma was hypnotizing, and it wasn't long before she caught my stare and smiled.

"Radhe, Radhe, Beta. Nam kya hai?" (Greetings, what is your name?)

"Radhe, Radhe" was a common greeting in the land of Krishna. It is said that Radha was Krishna's beloved, and by invoking her name in greetings, villagers express their desire to emulate the deep love she had for Lord Krishna.

"Nimi," I said shyly, trying not to stare at her.

"Pyari hai," (She's lovely) she said to my father.

I blushed, wanting to hide but also feeling a warmth in my belly from this woman's admiration and kindness.

Over the next few days, we returned to this *kirtan* gathering daily. My relationship with Didi grew nonverbally through smiles, sidelong glances, nods, and laughs. At the end of the week, my father approached her to see if she would come to our home so that we could host a *kirtan* gathering.

When she arrived, I was beyond excited. We had been planning this event for the entire week. Over the preceding few days, I had built a beautiful altar in our basement with saris draped from the ceiling, string lights along the borders, and plants and flowers adorning the platform. I cushioned the tiled floor with blankets to ensure that kirtan attendees were supported, covering them with white sheets the way I had seen at the gathering where I met Didi. I created a stage with wooden planks I found in the garage and topped them with a thick blanket and more white sheets, making a cozy stage from which Didi could lead the *kirtan*.

Didi spent the next two days getting settled into her routine in our home, and I did everything I could to make sure she was comfortable. Over time, she began to reach out to me first when she needed something. I felt a strong bond with her and was proud of how my actions had earned her trust and made her feel at ease.

As people arrived for the *kirtan* gathering, I led them to the kitchen for chai and snacks.

Didi called me up to her room. "Will you sing today?"

I felt a squeal beginning to arise within, and I pushed it back down, not wanting to sound overly excited.

I looked at her. "OK."

She smiled softly and nodded.

I left her room and went back downstairs to help my mother attend to the guests.

Soon, it was time for the *kirtan* to begin. My father, in his own excitement, scurried around, trying to ensure everything was in place. "Is Didi ready?" he asked me.

"I think so. Let's get everyone downstairs and then she'll come." A quiet sense of pride swelled within me as I spoke. I was beginning to see that my father often relied on me in these situations.

Slowly, guests trickled into the basement to find their places on the cushioned floor in front of the altar. Some chatted quietly with each other; others sat upright with their eyes closed in meditation; and others waited patiently, looking around the room. A hushed reverence filled the air as footsteps softened and voices dropped to a gentle murmur.

When Didi arrived downstairs, guests cleared the way for her to get to the front of the room. She seemed very introspective as she took her seat on stage and began the invocation prayer. I loved watching Didi sing, and the profound devotion she evinced was something I greatly admired and aspired to.

In between songs, Didi spoke about the beauty of unconditional love and the pleasure of surrendering ourselves to God in this way. Her words tugged on a longing that was deep within my own heart. I wanted to experience unconditional love. I hung on her every word, believing that each one held the key to unlocking something I was missing—the link between me and my desires.

When she asked me to sing, I nodded and began. As my voice filled the space, she played the harmonium, her notes harmonizing with mine. Her steady gaze as I sang created a transcendent sense of connection within me—like being perfectly aligned with something far beyond us, as though we were in sync with the heavens.

During a break, she and other attendees praised my voice, my devotion, and the way I had "maintained my culture despite living in the US." While I cherished the moments Didi and I shared, such compliments always made me feel uncomfortable. It felt weird to be commended for my strong emotions. I wanted to escape from the conversation but didn't want to seem rude.

Before the weekend-long gathering ended, we had scheduled another one for the following month, and Didi planned to stay with us until then. There were several guests who had requested that she come to their homes for an evening of *kirtan*, and it made sense for her to stay in town for these events. I went with her to each of the gatherings to both ensure that she was comfortable and to sing.

After the next *kirtan*, another was scheduled, and in this way, Didi stayed for another six months. I became more and more attached to her as she told me stories of her guru back in India, and I felt a growing urge to meet him stirring within me.

"The relationship with guru is even more reverent and special than that with God," she would tell me. "We can't see God, but we can see and touch our guru, so he is at an even higher place."

She sang to me:

"Guru Govind dono khade.

Kisko lagu paye?

Balihari Gurudeva Ki

Govind diyo dikhaye."

(Guru and God are standing together. We think to ourselves, who should we pay respects to first? I sacrifice myself for my Guru, as he has shown me God.)

This popular couplet by Kabir Das, a fifteenth-century Indian mystic and poet, became my own inner mantra in my desire to get closer to the divine.

I was determined to go to India and meet Didi's guru—to make him mine. Each day, I prayed to Lord Krishna to bring me closer to him and make the journey possible.

A few months later, my father received a letter from one of the women who had organized the very first *kirtan* where my father and I met Didi. She had recently been to India and met Didi's guru. In the letter, she warned my father that the guru in India had tried to rape her, claiming that this was the way of surrender and the ultimate relationship with the divine.

My father was furious. He confronted Didi, and she left before I even knew what had happened.

I didn't understand how my father could believe such ridiculous stories about Didi. *She had stayed in our home for six months . . . surely, we knew who she really was?*

"How dare you?" I glared at my father.

"Beta, you don't understand how dangerous this is!" My father looked at me with a mix of pleading and restrained anger, trying to control both himself and me.

"Then why did you have her stay here for so long?" I was heartbroken, but my anger had created a shell around the pieces.

"I didn't know!" The change in his voice was sudden. The softness that was there a moment ago was now replaced by bitterness. "How could I have known? I just found out, and I am doing what I need to do. Now, let's eat dinner and move on from this!" His voice was taut with anger and certainty, as if he believed that ending the discussion was the only solution.

"I don't want to eat," I retorted, storming off to my room and slamming the door behind me. I locked it for good measure.

I stood in my room, taking in my surroundings and thought, *this is my home from now on.*

Determined not to confront my father, I decided to stay in my room indefinitely. Throughout the day, I sat in front of my small altar, praying with fierce intensity.

Krishna, I am only wanting to be closer to YOU! So, if I'm on the wrong path, then show me! I'm doing this out of my love for YOU!

As the days went by, my father brought extended family from out of town to persuade me to let go of my attachment to Didi, but their efforts were futile. I became increasingly stubborn. Didi would call and only speak when I answered. During one of these calls, she gave me the number where she was staying and asked me to call her when I could. Since cell phones weren't yet available, I saved my lunch money to use the payphone at school to speak with her.

When we spoke, Didi would check on how I was doing and urge me to have faith. She also asked if my father had gotten any mail. Since he hadn't shared any details about the first letter—or any others he had received—I had no idea what had arrived. Didi wanted me to go through his mail to see if there was any correspondence related to her or her guru.

Wait . . . this doesn't feel right, my intuition nudged. I did not believe any of the things my father was being told, but why did I need to go through his mail to find the letters? *Who cares what people are saying?* I thought. But then Didi reminded me of the importance of committing to guru, and in that moment, my intuition was squashed. Her words were enough to override my inner voice. *Yes,* I thought. *I can do this.*

I waited until my parents were out to go into their bedroom. There was a filing cabinet against the back wall, and I knew that anything of importance that my father received would be in there. I searched, not really knowing what I was looking for. I found nothing. I shut the drawer, and it closed with the clang of a heavy tin can. A rumbling noise came from downstairs. *The garage door was opening!*

I tiptoed quickly down the hall toward my bedroom, hoping my parents wouldn't hear me as they came through the front door. My heart pounded in my chest, a blend of anxiety and unease settling over me. I hated the secrecy of what I was doing. I planned to tell Didi that I hadn't found anything and that I couldn't continue searching. By the time my mother came upstairs to check on me, my heartbeat had slowed, and I had collected myself.

"Nimi, your father wants to talk to you."

"OK." *Oh no, did they find out?* I padded down the stairs, finding my dad in the kitchen. I sat down on one of our dining chairs, waiting for him to speak.

"I'm going to see Babaji next week, and I want you to come with me."

"Who is *Babaji*?" I asked flatly.

"He's my guru."

"I have my own guru," I sneered defiantly. "Babaji isn't my guru."

My father sighed softly. "That's fine, Nimi. Just come and meet him. It can't hurt."

I was surprised by the gentleness in his voice. He seemed compassionate and loving, and I was not used to this side of my father.

Maybe Daddy's guru will understand and tell my father to let me follow Didi. The thought was intoxicating, and as I latched on to it, I began to form my plan.

"Fine, I'll go," I said, as I looked at him intentionally. I didn't let him see any evidence of the excitement I felt inside. I was angry, and I wanted him to feel that.

As I would find out much later, my father had gone to speak with his guru about his fears about Didi and the hold that she and her guru had over me. "I'm really worried about her," he'd shared. Babaji asked him to bring me to the next spiritual gathering he was leading in Washington, D.C. "I'll talk to her and let the Ramayana discourse do the rest."

My father was thrilled as it was not easy to get Babaji's time. He had hundreds of thousands of followers here in the US and millions back home in India. Getting private time with him was a big deal, and my father did not take that lightly.

I thought about my upcoming visit with Babaji. There were so many things I needed to tell him so that he would understand the whole story and (hopefully) scold my father for his behavior toward Didi and me. Though I didn't know the crowd sizes that followed Babaji, I knew that I wouldn't get much time with him, and I wasn't sure if that time would be alone or with my father.

How was I going to tell him everything I needed him to know?

I decided there would be too much to say, so the next day, I set aside an hour to write a letter to Babaji, giving him all the details he would need. I wanted him to see what was really happening and make sure he knew all of it before I met with him. This way, we'd be able to use our time to explain to my father how wrong he was in stopping me from following my own guru.

I sat down at my desk with a few sheets of blank paper in front of me. I would have to write this letter in Hindi as I didn't think this man could read English. I began to write, and though I wasn't sure if I had spelled words correctly or put the accents on letters appropriately, I decided to write unfiltered and then take time to edit the letter later.

I looked down at the two pages I had just written and was impressed with my writing. I had always loved the look of the Devanagari script, and it gave me so much joy to be able to write it.

I decided to put my letter away for a bit. The next day, I spent about two hours editing, taking pieces out and putting others in to ensure that Babaji understood how my father just didn't get Didi the way I did. I wanted him to know how angry I was that my father was messing up this special bond Didi and I had and that he was getting in the way of me connecting with her guru. Babaji needed to know that my father was getting in the way of my relationship with God!

Finally, I was satisfied. I folded the letter and sealed it in an envelope, placing it into the side pocket of the duffle bag I was packing for my upcoming trip.

***

The convention center was alive with the sounds of vibrant folk music and a sea of orange, green, and blue *lehengas* (a traditional Indian skirt) swirling gracefully as we entered. Thousands of people danced and sang, each one in a state of ecstatic devotion, all straining for a glimpse of the same man. I couldn't help but feel a deep curiosity about the sense of belonging these people shared. I wondered who this man was who inspired such a powerful connection.

I hesitated as my dad ushered us into the hall and toward the front. Suddenly, the crowd parted, and a man, surrounded by ten bodyguards, walked down the aisle toward the back of the room. We rushed to one side to get out of the way.

He was dressed entirely in yellow—a long tunic paired with a cloth wrapped around his waist, flowing to the floor like a skirt. About my father's age, maybe forty-five, he stood around five foot seven with a soft face that contrasted his confident, deliberate gait. In one hand, he carried a cloth printed with mantras in Sanskrit, the other arm swinging gently as he walked—each step landing with the assuredness of someone who knew the space was his.

The crowd erupted, screaming and cheering as if he were some sort of celebrity. When he got close to us, he seemed to recognize my dad and offered him a warm smile. Then his gaze shifted to me, and his smile widened. People nearby took notice; I could feel their eyes on me and I could hear their whispers as they leaned in to talk to their family members.

How the hell does this man—who no one can get within ten feet of—know my father? Does he know me? Why did he smile at me? How am I going to get my letter to him?

At that very moment, the stranger stopped and looked directly into my eyes. I shifted uncomfortably, feeling a mix of alarm and shyness.

This superstar of a man was smiling at me again.

The next morning, we got to the convention center before the discourse began. As we walked into the main hall, I was hit by the crispness of the air conditioning, the sight of brightly colored saris and *salwar kameezes* (long tunics with baggy pants), and the sounds of bangles and anklets jingling. In the back of the hall, children were running and playing in their traditional attire. Many in attendance sat on their blankets on the floor, saving spots near the stage for their families. Workers—identified by their badges—walked around, making sure that only VIPs sat in the sections reserved for them. *What makes someone a VIP?* I wondered.

Amid the bustling crowd, my attention was drawn to the enormous stage. At its center stood a seat that resembled a chariot straight out of a Hindu myth, seemingly prepared for Babaji. The backdrop was dominated by towering images of Hindu gods and goddesses, their presence overwhelming. It was an incredible sight, almost too much to absorb all at once.

My father led my mother and me to an area closer to the front. As soon as we found a spot that would fit the three of us, we sat down. We waited for the event to begin, and I took that time to observe the people sitting around us. They were speaking in their mother tongue, and there was a feeling of togetherness that impressed me. I was surprised by how elaborately the women were dressed. They were wearing heavy saris and *lehengas* covered in golden embroidery, sequins, and gems. Their jewelry was beautiful and even a bit gaudy, and their hair was intricately styled, as if they were attending a wedding.

Suddenly, the room fell quiet. I turned around to see what had silenced the crowd. Once again, Babaji walked from the back of the hall down the aisle toward the front, surrounded by a swarm of bodyguards. As they passed, people on either side of the path stood up with folded hands, their eyes moist and their heads bowed. Some stayed near the floor and reached out to try to touch the guru's feet as he walked by. The bodyguards blocked anyone from getting too close. Anyone who did was severely reprimanded.

After Babaji took his seat on the stage, there were several lengthy announcements and speeches. Finally, the music began. The sound of the violin was mesmerizing, and I immediately felt connected to my own heart as I closed my eyes to listen. Tears began to stream down my face, and I had no idea why. This music brought me closer to myself than I had felt in a long time. I allowed it to envelop me as I listened to the melodies and the mantras that were sung in the invocation prayer.

After Babaji's sermon, I made up my mind that I would find a way to get my letter to him. As soon as the final prayer was over and people began standing up, I reached into my bag and pulled out the envelope. I glanced at my dad, who seemed to know what I was about to do and nodded. I ran to the back of the hall by the exit and stood there waiting for Babaji to pass by. My heart was beating fast from both the running and the anticipation I felt about meeting this man again. Spending these last few hours listening to him, I felt as if I had been put in a trance.

Over the next few minutes, many more people seemed to have the same idea I did, and they began crowding around the exit. *Get out of my way,* I thought, pushing my way forward competitively. *I was here first, and I have something to give him.*

I stood up and made sure that no one was able to get in front of me. I looked down the aisle of the main hall and saw the same group of men ushering Babaji back through the hall. I had my letter ready and felt my hands begin to tremble. *Would he even notice me? What if one of those men yells at me or swats me away?*

As Babaji drew closer, I focused on him, hoping that he would glance my way. Seconds before he reached me, he looked at me and smiled. I held out my letter, and he reached out to take it. *He got it!* I was flustered for a moment and stood still, observing the crowd rush past. From a distance, I watched as he got into the car waiting for him and immediately began opening my envelope. *Oh my god! He's reading it!*

I felt a rush of adrenaline as I walked back to find my parents. I wondered how my father would react, but his usual seriousness had melted into awestruck wonder. He was positively beaming.

"Good job, Nimi. Good job." The fact that I had made contact with Babaji seemed to be more important than anything else.

***

We pulled up to the house where Babaji was staying, and I was astonished at how many people were there. It took us a while to find parking due to the volume of cars. We walked for about twenty minutes to get to the house along with several other families who were walking there as well—some reciting mantras that Babaji had taught, and others expressing their excitement to see him. Though I had not experienced more than a day of his discourse and even though I had a guru of my own, I felt butterflies in my stomach as we approached.

So many people. Sitting on the steps, standing in the driveway and on the front lawn, children playing in the street . . . there were people everywhere.

My dad made his way up the driveway and spoke to a man at the front door. Dad then turned around and gestured excitedly for us to come in. We hurried as fast as we could, weaving through the crowd. The moment we reached the top of the stairs and the front door, we were ushered into an overcrowded living room. I looked down to find a spot to place my next step, but there was nothing. Each step I took required someone to move or get up to make space. Finally, we made it across the room and were welcomed to a small patch of floor. We sat down, trying to take up as little space as we could. I hugged my knees tightly to my chest. Around us, people were singing hymns and mantras as they waited. I was used to sitting on the floor, but this was a whole new test of endurance. My legs and hips ached from being so cramped.

About five minutes after we arrived, a large man announced that Babaji was coming and told us to make room for him to walk through. It was as if the seas parted. There was no space, and yet—like a wave—people flowed into every corner and crevice to create a passageway for Babaji. There was an almost childlike devotion in the way people watched him—eyes wide, bodies leaning forward, as if hoping for a single glance in return.

The guru had barely sat down before he stood up again and motioned for my dad to follow him. I was confused. *What about all these people? How well did my dad know this man? Out of all these people, Babaji wanted to see my dad?*

My father looked back at us and gave us that same excited hand wave, urging us to follow him. Carefully, we got up, trying not to step on people on the way. I felt a pang of guilt walking past those who had been waiting uncomfortably to see Babaji for so long. I could feel their stares as we followed my dad and his guru upstairs to a quiet room.

Babaji sat on a rocking chair while we sat on the floor by his feet. For a few moments, an awkward silence hung in the air. I nervously traced the patterns in the multi-colored rug with my fingers, avoiding eye contact and staring intently at the floor.

Finally, Babaji spoke. "I read your letter."

He looked at me and paused. "It's so good that you desire Krishna so much and that you are so aware of your religion and culture."

I looked up, initially unaware that he was speaking to me. His eyes locked on to mine, and his piercing gaze made me momentarily lose all sense of who I was.

"You are very young, so be careful," he continued.

I'm not sure what happened in that moment, but it was clear that something had shifted. Many family members had tried to tell me to "be careful" with regard to Didi and her guru. I had so much to say to them when they told me this. I argued and said they were insane to buy into such garbage. And yet, this guy, who I hardly know, tells me to "be careful," and all I can say is "OK"?

It felt as if someone had done surgery on my heart and mind that day. Any attachment I had to Didi was gone. Strangely, I no longer thought of her, missed her, or even heard from her again.

For the rest of the discourse, I listened intently. I lost myself in the music. I repeatedly tried to position myself where Babaji would notice me and smile. There was something inside of me that felt emboldened and loved each time he did. Every morning, we woke early to get to the hall in time to save our seats in the front. After situating our blanket, we would then drive thirty minutes to the house where Babaji was staying to be able to sit with him and about a hundred other people for ten minutes. Then, we rushed back to the hall and spent the day there listening to his music and teachings. After the discourse, we quickly had dinner and rushed back to the house once again to catch a glimpse of Babaji and perhaps sit in his presence among the crowd for a few minutes. This went on for an entire week. While the days were full and we were exhausted at night, we did it enthusiastically. We were starstruck and completely caught up in all the fanfare. It would take twenty years for us to realize how hypnotized we actually were.

4

Infatuation

In the following years, I attended all of Babaji's spiritual gatherings in the US and even went to India a few times to listen to him there. I tried to incorporate his teachings into my life by reciting the mantras he taught, reading the scriptures, and taking a vow of silence for one day each week. The altar I had in my room now had Babaji's picture on it, and I would often long for the next time I would be able to see him. Each time I attended a spiritual gathering, the last day and evening was a time of mourning because Babaji would soon be leaving. When I think back on this time, I recall how intense everything was, and yet it was an intensity I craved. It was as though this was something I had permission to feel, and, therefore, I was determined to *really* feel it.

I made friends who became like family within the community. What we shared was so sacred that it often felt as if these friends were closer than any family I had ever known. We sat together during discourses. We cried and laughed together. When Babaji would sing folk songs, we would get up and dance. At other times, we would change the words of Bollywood love songs and sing them to Babaji during the evening visiting hours. When he looked at us, we'd duck to hide our heads, but the giggles were obvious. When he giggled back, we'd squeal in delight.

Two years after I first met Babaji, I began to notice small tattoos adorning the inner forearms of some of his followers. The tattoos read "*Ram*" in Devanagari script, identical to one that Babaji himself bore in the same spot. I desperately wanted to be part of this inner circle. Despite being only sixteen, my parents granted me permission when I asked. I then approached Babaji and requested that he write "*Ram*" on my arm so I could have it tattooed. He obliged, and, ecstatically, I went to the tattoo parlor with a few friends to make it permanent. Carrying Babaji's handwriting with me at all times brought me immense comfort.

Babaji often remarked about his own tattoo that, being only human, he didn't trust himself to always remember Ram—the name of God—so he wrote it in his blood. This sentiment resonated deeply with me. The following year, I returned to Babaji and asked if he would write his own name in my blood, so I could ensure I'd never forget him—my guru, the one guiding me toward God.

During these spiritual gatherings, we made it our business to find out about every place Babaji was going to visit. We made sure we got there first so that we could stand in front of the crowd to catch a glimpse of him.

In America, the crowds for Babaji's teachings were large, but when I visited him in India, I was utterly unprepared for what I saw. The spiritual gatherings were held in enormous tents, yet they could hardly contain the ocean of people who came to listen. Hundreds of thousands—sometimes even millions—gathered, their devotion palpable, their voices rising in chants of his name. Those who couldn't squeeze inside stood on rooftops or pressed against barriers, clustered around loudspeakers, desperate to catch even a single word.

At times the sheer density of the crowd was overwhelming. There was no way through—it was as if the bodies around me had merged into an unmovable, living wall. People stood shoulder to shoulder, the press of bodies leaving little room to breathe. The air buzzed with anticipation, thick with the scent of incense, sweat, and the dust kicked up by thousands of shuffling feet.

Because we had come from America, we were granted access to the front—a privilege that shielded us from the chaos but also gave us a striking perspective. When we stood and looked back, the crowd seemed endless, stretching beyond the horizon. From any one spot, we could never fully grasp the entirety of it; everywhere we turned, the mass of people extended farther than the eye could see. It was awe-inspiring and humbling, a true testament to the power of devotion that had drawn so many to this one man, this one voice.

We often visited Babaji during Guru Purnima, a sacred full moon day in late June or early July when Hindus honor and celebrate their spiritual teachers. The heat at that time of year in India is oppressive, and the small village where Babaji stayed would transform overnight, swelling with crowds so immense that the streets became impassable. We waited for hours in the suffocating heat just hoping for a fleeting glimpse of him. The wait was excruciating, but we reminded ourselves that we were among the fortunate ones. So many others had walked for miles only to be turned away when the crowds became too large to control.

Coming from the US, we never had to endure the same struggles as those who had sacrificed everything just to be in Babaji's orbit. We carried that privilege with awareness, knowing that while we were given a direct path to him, others stood under the burning sun, pressed against the outer barriers, hoping to feel his energy, if only for a moment.

But even with this privilege, the sheer intensity of the experience could be overwhelming. The heat, the crowds, the long hours of waiting—it was enough to push the body past its limits. On one Guru Purnima, I learned this firsthand.

The intense heat took its toll on my body. Although I remained determined to see Babaji on this special day, my body couldn't take it, and I fainted. My parents quickly poured water over my face, cooling me down until I regained consciousness. Despite my body's protest, we remained in line, all of us unwilling to miss this sacred chance. As I finally walked past Babaji, I was rewarded by his radiant smile. There was a knowing in his expression, as if he understood my struggle and recognized my persistence. In that moment, the pain and discomfort melted away, leaving only the sweetness of his acknowledgment.

My entire life's focus became about Babaji and everything he had to say. My prayers focused on him, and before I began anything new, I would call him to ask for blessings. This was no small feat, as calling India in 1989 required several phone numbers and a lot of patience. It could take anywhere from a few hours to sometimes days to get through, and then we were lucky if he was available to speak.

Every year, I celebrated Karva Chauth by fasting and praying to find a good husband. After meeting Babaji, each year, my Karva Chauth was dedicated to him as I prayed for his long life.

During my senior year of high school, there was a spiritual gathering happening in Gangotri, a small town in the Garhwal Himalayas. Only two hundred people were permitted to go due to the challenging journey required to get to this town, which was considered to be a pilgrimage site and the source of the holy Ganges River. Babaji was personally selecting the participants, and I was ecstatic to find out that my name was on the list. When the logistics for the trip were finalized, we learned that it would occur at the same time as both the final show choir performance of my senior year and my high school graduation. While there was a part of me that was disappointed, I quickly buried that feeling and rejoiced at being chosen to go see my guru. I let my teachers know and made arrangements to take all my finals before I left. I was sad that I would miss graduating with my friends and celebrating with them during our final performance, but the joy I felt at going on this trip somehow canceled out any of that sorrow.

Babaji was the center of my life. Anything was worth giving up for him. The cost of this mindset would make itself known decades later.

Part Two

Shadows

"Do not look for healing at the feet of those who broke you."

— Rupi Kaur

5

The Dream

So much had changed over the past decade since Babaji entered my life. He wasn't just a mentor—he became my purpose, my joy, and the one thing I felt I was finally doing right. My father, who rarely approved of the people I cared about or the things I loved, not only accepted Babaji but had been the one to introduce me to him. And now, in Babaji, I had discovered the father figure I'd yearned for all my life—someone who didn't just make me feel worthy but made me feel like more than enough. On the rare occasions when he visited our home and made sure others knew he'd be spending time with us, I felt as though I were deeply important to him.

"I have to go to Nimi's house," he'd say, signaling that it was *me* he wanted to visit.

When he had to choose who would be attending the spiritual gathering in the Himalayas, he chose me!

When I'd give him my letters, I could tell that he had read them when we next spoke. I mattered, my thoughts mattered . . . and they mattered to someone who had millions of people wanting his attention.

Babaji was incredibly generous with his guidance, and the warmth he radiated filled me from the inside, making me feel not just truly special but truly alive.

Sometimes, Babaji would test me, pretending not to know me or snapping at me in front of others. In these moments, I felt entirely deficient. My happiness or despair seemed to depend completely on his whims. And yet, I still sought his recognition and approval. I decided that I wanted to change my name. Nimi held no real meaning for me, and the idea of receiving a new name from Babaji felt like a sacred initiation.

When I first asked him to give me a new name, he told me to return the following week; by then, we would be in Gangotri. So, during the Gangotri spiritual gathering, I went to him, expecting the moment I had been waiting for. But when I finally stood before him, he looked me in the eyes and said, "How much time do you think I have?" His words were not a question. They were cold and final.

The rapidly shifting moods were confusing, but before I could wrap my head around one wild swing, he'd switch back to the loving, comforting guru I knew and adored. And so, I rationalized it all away, telling myself that he was spending all this energy on me . . . *Me*. I accepted and trusted the love and generous teachings of equanimity he was offering, always telling myself, "He's doing this all for me. If he didn't care, he wouldn't be pushing me to become my best self."

It was hard at times, but I couldn't see any other way. No one else was willing to help me grow with the compassion he offered. So, I leaned in harder, doing everything I could to show my devotion. Babaji often asked us to commit to repeating specific mantras several times a day to help us through challenging times and build our faith. Whenever I felt pushed away from Babaji, I would whisper these mantras under my breath—for courage, for reassurance, and to remind myself of all that he was doing for me.

The discourse in Gangotri was unlike anything I had ever experienced. Listening to my beloved guru's voice in such a holy place felt otherworldly. Sometimes it seemed as though an unspoken "Om" vibrated in the wind, carried through the Himalayas. The mountains, ancient and unmoving, stood as silent witnesses to every word he spoke.

But beyond the spiritual awe, we also lived the experience—fully. We stayed in an old wooden hut, in a room on the top floor, where every creak in the floorboards echoed. There was no place to bathe, so we held up saris around each other, taking turns washing ourselves with buckets of water. Hair washing required strategy—planned in advance, always in the warmth of the afternoon—because the morning and night air was far too cold for a cold bath. It was a simple, makeshift way of living, yet it bonded us in a way nothing else could. Some might have seen it as rough, even unbearable, but to us, it felt like part of the journey, an experience we'd never forget.

Each morning, we gathered on the banks of the Ganges, the river's fast-moving current creating a symphony of rushing water beneath Babaji's voice. For three and a half hours, we sat cross-legged, listening as he carefully selected just a few lines from the Ramayana—lines that would anchor his teachings for the entire nine-day spiritual gathering. This time, he spoke of King Bhagirath's relentless penance at Gangotri, the devotion that brought Ganga (Ganges River) down from the heavens to cleanse the ashes of his ancestors. His words wove through the air like the river itself, carrying lessons of surrender, perseverance, and the discipline of devotion.

Shortly after the spiritual gathering in the Himalayas, Babaji came to the US for his yearly trip and planned to visit our home. It was during this visit that he gave me my new name, Gangotri.

***

I can't believe it's only one more day until I get married.

I stared at myself in the mirror of the upstairs bedroom as I brushed my hair, a myriad of thoughts running through my mind.

It was the day before I was to marry my future husband. I was excited, scared, unsure, and nervous. Vick and I had met each other at least ten years earlier. I remembered him coming to Babaji's spiritual gatherings, and although we were in the same friend circles, we had never really had a full conversation.

After completing my MBA, I had come to India with my mother to spend time with Babaji. When we arrived at the ashram, I was excited to see who else was there. It was always so much fun to hang out with other devotees my age.

I dropped my things off in the room my mother and I were assigned and went out to explore. The complex was large, with all the rooms opening to an inner courtyard and garden. Down the hall, familiar voices and laughter spilled from a half-open door. I knocked lightly, and Vick swung it open.

For a moment, he just stood there, staring at me. His eyes scanned my face, his expression unreadable. The intensity of it made me shift on my feet. *Was he surprised to see me? Confused? Something else?* I wasn't sure, but his staring made me even more aware of the others in the room behind him. I could hear movement and hushed voices, but Vick's presence filled the doorway, commanding the moment.

"Gangotri!" he exclaimed, his voice much louder than necessary.

"Hey, Gangotri!" I turned slightly and saw another familiar face from previous years smiling at me. "When did you arrive?"

I exchanged a few pleasantries with the group, still feeling the heat of Vick's stare, and then excused myself to return to my room and freshen up for the evening.

Over the next few weeks, Vick made an effort to spend as much time as possible with me. At first, it felt weird, and I was not at all interested. As time went on, however, I became enamored by the fact that he liked me, and eventually I convinced myself that I had feelings for him as well. He was a very devoted disciple of Babaji, which made him more attractive. After all, Babaji was everything to me. I couldn't imagine living life without him as my guide.

We had been in India for nearly three months when Vick asked Babaji for his blessing to marry me. To our delight, Babaji agreed, and the preparations for a simple wedding at the ashram quickly took shape. Years before, my father had purchased a small house that was to be built in Babaji's village, imagining it as both a retreat for us and a future home for himself and my mother after retirement. By some perfect alignment of the stars, the house was completed just in time for the wedding. We moved our things in and began setting up our new home.

As the week of the wedding approached, family members began arriving, their presence making everything suddenly feel very real. The house filled with voices, movement, and the chaotic energy of last-minute preparations. Yet even with all the excitement, an uneasiness settled inside me, quiet but persistent.

The weather in Babaji's village was hot and humid, the air thick with the scent of blooming flowers and damp earth. The lush surroundings should have felt beautiful and grounding—but instead, they seemed heavy, almost suffocating.

Despite the serene atmosphere, I couldn't shake the feeling that something was off. My mother tried to appear excited about her daughter getting married, but beneath her façade, I sensed her disappointment. I knew she was pushing aside her doubts—just as I was.

In my desperation to break free from my mother's control, I had allowed her to be disrespected. She disapproved of the way Vick and I were together, believing that dating before marriage was unacceptable. In her presence, I was torn between deep shame and a defiant urge to challenge her beliefs.

Vick, however, didn't just dismiss her opinions—he spoke to her with a sharpness that made it clear he didn't think her words carried weight. He twisted Babaji's teachings in ways that suited him, especially when they contradicted what my mother said or wanted. If she reminded us of the rules, he would deliberately break them— ignoring her authority, brushing off her concerns, and encouraging me to do the same with a smirk, as if it were all just harmless rebellion. And yet, looking back, I see the hypocrisy so clearly. For all the weight he placed on his own mother's words—her feelings, her needs—my mother's were met with casual disregard. I tolerated it, even used it to deepen my own defiance, as if his rebellion could drown out my guilt.

Even though something in me felt uneasy, I clung to the hope that this was what I'd been waiting for. I had longed for this moment my whole life—surely this was the answer to all those fasts, all those prayers.

As I ran my heavy black brush through my hair, a thorny memory surfaced. Just a year prior, I'd been in almost this same situation. At the time, I'd been dating a guy from New York who I'd met online. Kaushal and I had fallen for each other fast, and months later, he proposed to me over the phone. I'd been ecstatic. To be honest, I wasn't really sure I loved him, but the thought of being someone's wife was so intoxicating that I immediately said yes.

A few days later, however, my bubble burst when he called back to tell me that he was withdrawing his proposal. As he later explained, his mother had read our birth charts, and we were "not compatible."

Now, one year later, here I was . . . about to get married again.

I stared at myself in the mirror, watching my deep brown eyes staring back.

At my core, I knew Vick wasn't right for me, but I was focused on the fear of not finding a husband, not on my own intuition.

Stop worrying, I told myself. *Babaji is coming to visit tomorrow. I'll get a chance to talk to him before the wedding, and all will be well.*

When I woke up the next day, serenity surrounded me. The heaviness didn't matter, and the shame felt far away, because soon Babaji would be there, in our home.

He felt like the voice of my conscience. Just knowing I had his approval gave me a sense of inner confidence that nothing else could match—not even validation from my own parents. When I earned Babaji's approval, it was as if a quiet strength settled within me, unlike anything I had felt before.

We prepared for Babaji's arrival by cleaning the house and preparing *pakoras* (fried vegetables coated in chickpea flour). Mangoes, lychees, and fruits of all sorts were cut and displayed beautifully on silver platters. We set out the bowl we would use to wash his feet with water from the Ganges River. He was to be treated like a king when he arrived.

The room felt cool and refreshing, a stark contrast to the muggy heat outside. His chair was draped in a freshly washed white sheet, with another neatly folded at the base for his feet to rest upon. I carefully rubbed a sandalwood stick against a stone, gathering the fragrant paste that I would later apply to his feet. Woody notes filled the air, adding to the calm, sacred atmosphere.

When he arrived, he looked at me and smiled. As always, this gesture filled my heart and let me know that I was enough—worthy of his glance and his smile.

He was guided to the room where he would sit to have his meal.

I was allowed in to talk with Babaji privately. I sat on the floor in front of him, looking up into his eyes, silent for a few moments.

"I'm scared," I finally said, quietly. He smiled knowingly.

In the silence, I reached forward and touched his feet gently. It is said in my culture that to get to the wisdom of a wise man, you must start at their feet, and Babaji's were smooth and cool. I felt both self-conscious and grateful to have this opportunity. Millions of people came to get just a glimpse of Babaji, and here I was, alone in a room with him, allowed to touch his feet without being pushed away. I had his attention all to myself.

As I sat there, I thought about how I craved the security and warmth of a father figure. While my own father had come for the wedding, I had never been able to experience him this way. In his presence, I always felt on edge, as if I were disappointing him.

Now, as I looked up at Babaji, I felt that security. His smile was warm and welcoming.

"Can I have a hug?" I asked.

I couldn't believe those words had just left my lips. People flocked from all over the world to get a glimpse of this man, and I was asking for an embrace? My heart felt like a drum beating through my chest as I began to tremble.

He paused, letting the seconds pass, each one feeling like an eternity.

"Will you be able to handle it?" he asked.

Perplexed, I stared at him. *Of course,* I thought. *Why would I not be able to handle his embrace? He was the epitome of fatherly love. Why would that be hard to handle?*

I nodded.

He got up and asked me to turn around. The tone of his voice was different. The gentle, compassionate voice I had heard before had transformed into a tone of forceful authority.

I was confused. *Is there a right way to hug that I wasn't aware of?*

He wrapped his arms around me and began to kiss my neck.

My skin prickled, my head suddenly foggy. *Umm . . . what is happening?*

My mind began racing. *Is this what I asked for? Why is he doing this?*

His hands cupped my breasts, and he began to squeeze.

I was stunned. I couldn't figure out how to deal with both my chaotic mind and this man's hands.

How can I be doubting Babaji???

The next few moments were a blur, and then from within me came a voice. *Surrender . . . He knows so much more than you do. Just surrender.*

So, I leaned my head back onto his shoulder and let him kiss my neck more as he continued to fondle my breasts.

He turned me around and brought his hand to my chin. He leaned in and kissed me. As he leaned back and looked at me, I must have appeared completely dumbfounded because he smiled and began to chuckle.

I'm not sure what happened next, but I feared my own mind and feelings. I worried that they would betray the one person in my life who I trusted the most, and I couldn't let that happen.

When he was done, he fixed his clothes and stood up, ready to leave.

"Don't talk about this with anyone. It could get very difficult for me if you do," he warned, without looking at me.

After he left, I wasn't sure what to do with myself. My mind was numb, and I didn't want to be around anyone. That night was my *mehndi* (henna) ceremony, and I worried about how I would get myself through it—whether I'd be able to mask the weight of the afternoon or if everyone would see right through me.

My legs felt like bricks as I made my way upstairs to my room: a bare space, with concrete floors, two cots, and a small dresser. I lay on one of the cots, staring blankly at the uneven, bumpy ceiling.

What was I supposed to do with this? I couldn't reconcile the sharp contradiction between my body's unmistakable warning that something was deeply wrong and the revered place Babaji held in my life and my family's life. The clash of these realities left me reeling in a dizzying whirlwind as my mind scrambled to create some semblance of safety. *Maybe I'm special?* I wondered, though skepticism clung to the thought like a shadow. *Maybe that's why he did it?*

There was no peace to be found in the storm of complex thoughts and emotions swirling within me. As I lay there, grappling with the weight of it all, I began questioning my own spiritual perception—my ability to truly see and understand the actions of my guru. A faint thread of relief flickered to life with the notion that perhaps it did all make sense but that my limited comprehension kept me from grasping it fully.

I held on to this thought, and it allowed me to compartmentalize the morning's events so that I could show up for the rest of the day. It was time to get ready for my mehndi ceremony. I wore my bright orange *salwar kameez*, as it resembled the color of the henna that was to be applied in preparation for the wedding. Growing up, there were so many aspects of my future wedding I'd looked forward to. I'd dreamt of this moment, of the intricate patterns of henna that would adorn my hands and feet. Even through the doubt I felt deep down, I also felt a bubbling sense of excitement.

As I left my bedroom and walked downstairs, I was greeted by the laughter and voices of all the women and girls who had gathered for the evening's events. I greeted each one as I passed them, some with smiles and others with hugs. I walked through the house to the front porch and sat on the swing hanging from the ceiling. The artist, Paru, who was to do my henna, prepared the lemon sugar water to help the paste stick to my skin. It was important to make sure that the paste stayed on long enough to leave a deep and dark stain on my limbs.

It is said that the darker the stain of a bride's mehndi on her wedding day, the more love she will receive from her mother-in-law. That love isn't just symbolic—it matters. For an Indian daughter-in-law stepping into a new home, that love can determine everything. Without it, she may find herself lost, constantly questioning her place, shrinking to fit in or striving endlessly to be enough. The love of a mother-in-law isn't just a blessing—it's a lifeline.

As Paru began to create beautiful swirls and paisley designs on my hands, a few other artists began to decorate the hands of the other girls and women. The guests sat on vibrant cushions on the floor, facing the artists who worked intently on their hands. Everyone was dressed in bright, colorful outfits that added to the cheerful energy of the gathering. Laughter and lively conversation mingled in the air as the artists continued their work, fully focused, yet immersed in the warmth of the celebration around them.

The purpose of this ritual is to bring auspiciousness to the wedding and to celebrate the bride, but as I looked around, I realized how lonely I felt. None of my close friends were there. Instead, there were girls who just happened to be staying in the ashram at the same time. A few of them were good friends of my fiancé, so I felt obliged to engage in their friendship. Instinctively however, I did not trust them. Early on, as I had tried to befriend them, I found myself unable to create a bond with any level of depth. The more I spoke to them, the more I found myself worried about what I looked like and what others were thinking of me. I felt lost and disconnected from myself, though I didn't realize it at the time.

As I look back, the need for sisterhood was something I had always felt and longed for. I would often convince myself of a deeper connection than I really had in order to satisfy this desire.

What's wrong? I wondered. *Why am I not able to relax and enjoy my own wedding celebrations?*

I was uncomfortable. And I felt haunted by both the events of the morning and the expectation that I should be excited.

After the henna ceremony, I spent the rest of the evening alone with my thoughts. For years, I had pictured this night so differently—imagining the joy of sharing my excitement with my fiancé, talking on the phone and dreaming about the future we'd create together. Instead, I was locked in an invisible battle, trying to silence the voice deep within me that whispered something wasn't right. I struggled to convince myself that everything was as it should be, that the choices I'd made and the faith I'd placed were unshakable truths. The inner conflict twisted and turned, refusing to let me rest, until exhaustion finally claimed me, and I slipped into an uneasy sleep.

***

When I awoke the next morning, it took me a few moments to feel the gravity of what had happened the day before. I thought about what this morning would be like so many times throughout my life. I'd be excited yet serene as I got myself ready to begin a new life.

I'm not sure if what I actually felt was more excitement or fear, as they both feel similar in my body. I intentionally pushed away the thoughts and questions that flooded my mind and focused on getting ready.

Downstairs, in the kitchen, I propped myself up on the counter and turned the gas stove on. I took turns hovering my henna-covered hands and feet over the flame so the dried paste and my skin could take in the heat and darken the color it would leave behind. I then took a butter knife to scrape off the remaining flakes that had stuck. I wasn't supposed to wash my hands and feet yet as this would stop the color from deepening.

Afterward, I waited about an hour before taking a shower. As I got dressed, I could hear the makeup and hair artists arriving downstairs. Soon, they came up and began working on me. My hair was swept into an elegant bun, and my makeup, though delicate, was far more dramatic than what I'd wear on any normal day. They carefully placed decorative *bindis* around my eyes and helped drape my sari. Heavy gold jewelry adorned me from head to toe—my neck, ears, head, waist, arms, and ankles all glittered. The jewelry alone felt as if it outweighed me, and walking became a small challenge.

It was time to go downstairs. I walked slowly so as not to trip on the nine yards of fabric gracefully draped around my body. As I entered the sitting room, everyone turned around with "oohhs" and "aahhs." I sat on the porch swing and the photographer began taking pictures. At first it was just me, and then various family members took turns posing with me.

As I got into the car to go to the ashram where the wedding was to take place, a small voice deep inside wondered what I was getting myself into. *"Shut up,"* I heard a louder and more authoritative voice within me say. *"You are going to mess everything up. Just sit down and shut up!"*

So, I did. I sat down and allowed myself to be driven to the ashram in the village, silencing the softer yet deeper voice inside me. When we arrived, I was led to a small room near the courtyard where the ceremony would take place. I had to be hidden, while Vick sat out in the open, waiting for things to begin.

After what seemed like a few hours, I heard the loud clank of Babaji's sandals. He entered the room and looked at me with a smile. I searched for some sort of acknowledgment of what had happened just the day before. There was nothing. I stared blankly and touched his feet as was expected. The reverence I usually felt when offering my respects seemed to be distant.

The thought came back: *I'm not spiritually aware enough to understand what happened. Just trust and all will be well.*

During the wedding, mantras were recited, and we walked around the fire as it witnessed us taking the seven steps that represent the seven Hindu vows of marriage. Afterward, we sat in front of Babaji, and he asked Vick what *we* wanted as our wedding gift. I was now non-existent except for my place as my husband's wife. Vick thought for a moment, and then, without speaking to me, said that he wanted to share our guru's last name. While Babaji was shocked, he agreed. My last name was now changed to Babaji's. We paid our respects and walked to the dining hall area to eat lunch with our families. After the simple meal of lentils, rice, and vegetables, we headed back to the house where Vick and his family were staying. I was now to stay with them as they were now my family.

That evening, we went to visit Babaji again at his home. We sat in his yard as he swung on his swing. There were occasional words with the men in the family. Thoughts of the previous day swirled in my head as I looked around for evidence that something was different. I'm not sure what I was expecting, but it felt impossible that things could continue just as they had been before yesterday. I sat alone with my thoughts and growing anxiety. Confusion and wonder, mixed with a bit of annoyance, all seemed to swirl together inside of me, forming a cloudy sense of reality. *How could he sit there as if nothing had changed?* His swing squeaked as it rocked back and forth in the silence. I felt his gaze every so often. When I looked up, his stare was blank. *What the hell is he thinking?* I couldn't tell, and I began to wonder if something was wrong with me.

That night, as my husband and I were getting ready for our first night together as a married couple, I realized I couldn't hold it in anymore.

As I looked in the mirror and applied cream to my face, I knew I had to say something.

"I need to talk to you," I said.

"OK, about what?" he asked.

"Yesterday, when Babaji came to my house to see me, something happened."

He stopped and turned to look at me, excitement in his eyes.

"What happened?" he asked.

I knew Vick was expecting me to tell him of some sort of spiritual miracle, and I wondered if that was indeed what I had to tell him.

"Who do you think Babaji is?" I asked.

He looked at me, confused. "He's *Sadguru Bhagawan*."

Sadguru Bhagawan means God, the true guru.

"Yeah, but do you think he is an incarnation?" I asked.

"What are you saying?" His eyes narrowed.

"I'm wondering if he is Krishna," I said.

"Gangotri, say what you are trying to say."

"He . . . " I paused, my stomach clenching. "He touched me." Slowly, I opened up, telling him about the hug I'd asked for, and everything that happened afterwards. How I wasn't sure what to do . . . what it meant . . . or how I should feel.

Before me, Vick's face transformed from excitement to confusion to fury. He was livid. I watched as the angles of his face sharpened, his chest puffed, and his body tightened. His eyes narrowed as he looked at me with disgust.

"We have to get this straight. We'll talk to him tomorrow." His voice was uncomfortably calm.

I knew I wasn't supposed to tell Vick, and I was terrified of what it would be like to talk to Babaji about it, never mind with Vick doing the asking. *Please don't do this!* my insides pleaded. The words got stuck. I feared that if I said them, he would doubt my intentions.

I felt a tight knot in my stomach, growing with every passing moment. There was no way around this. The truth was out, and now Vick was going to talk to Babaji about it. I wasn't sure what would happen; I only knew that it would not be good—especially for me.

It was our wedding night, and my husband got into bed, turned over, and closed his eyes. I stood there for a moment, unsure of what to do.

"Go to sleep," he said. "Tomorrow is going to be a long day."

The next morning, I awoke and got ready. As a new bride, I was expected to look like one, dressed in bright, new clothes with some of my wedding jewelry. It was hot, and the clothes and jewelry stuck to me the minute I put them on.

We went downstairs for breakfast and ate with Vick's parents before heading to the ashram to meet Babaji.

When it was our turn to speak to him, he called us over to a private area so that no one could hear what we were saying. He smiled at us and nodded as we bowed down to touch his feet.

Vick started, "Babaji, are you Krishna?"

My heart sank. I knew Babaji was not going to like that question.

"What?" Babaji asked, sounding annoyed.

"Gangotri told me about your visit with her before our wedding, and I was wondering if she belongs to you?" Vick said.

Babaji's face grew tense, his expression hardening. "Is this what you spent your first night as a couple discussing?" he demanded, in a tone I had never heard from him before. I could sense a simmering rage just beneath the surface, ready to erupt. He got up, kicked off his wooden sandals—which made a loud thwack as they hit the marble floor—and stormed off to a private room in the back. I was sure that everyone had heard the thundering sound.

Vick gave me a disgusted sneer that said, *Now look what you've done!*

With a similar expression of disgust on his face, Babaji's brother escorted us to the other side of the ashram.

Vick's parents approached us, their glares boring into me. "What did you *do*?"

Then, my parents. "What did you do to make Babaji so angry?"

"We've never seen him so angry before!"

I didn't know what I had done. I only knew that there was something happening that I did not understand, and I had made a mess of it all. My thoughts went back to the man, my father's friend, who made me feel uncomfortable while he was supposed to be teaching me Babaji's native language. When I had told my father about that incident, it wasn't just his response that unsettled me—it was the weight of everything beneath it. I was expected to dismiss what I felt in my body and focus on the man's intentions, as if harm only counted if it was deliberate. But men like him didn't need to intend anything. They moved through the world unchecked, so used to getting away with things that they didn't bother considering how their actions might land. *Why are the intentions and reputations of others worth more than what I feel in my own body?*

And yet, my purity was held as the highest virtue. It didn't add up; none of it made sense.

The only thing I knew for sure was that Babaji was my guru, and I believed he understood things far beyond what I could ever comprehend. In the face of everyone's disgust toward me, this thought crystallized as truth—it gave me something to hold on to, something that allowed me to sit with it all, even when it felt unbearable.

Despite the confusion and hurt, this experience didn't diminish my devotion to Babaji. If anything, it widened the distance between who I was and the pedestal I had placed him on. The weight of my unworthiness wrapped around me like an endless tide, pulling me under.

This was all it took to silence me—both my voice and my inner self. For the next decade, I lived with my true thoughts and feelings buried so deep that I could no longer feel or hear them.

6

The Good Girl

When Vick, my in-laws, and I arrived at their home in London, we were greeted by over 100 people gathered to celebrate and congratulate us on our wedding. I was rushed inside by several women who helped me change from my travel clothes back into my wedding sari so that I could reenter the home as a new bride. Everyone there was a follower of Babaji, and they welcomed us by singing and chanting songs that he would often sing in his discourses. Once I was dressed, I was led to sit at the front of the crowd around a *havan kund* (a ceremonial brick fire pit used for prayers). We began repeating mantras and offering ghee to the fire, praying that we would become a family that would embody devotion to our guru and to the ideals modeled by Lord Rama, the mythical incarnation of God portrayed in the ancient Hindu epic, The Ramayana. The mood was joyful, and during this celebration, despite all the shame, fear, and sadness I had felt just days before, I thought maybe we would be OK.

After the party, Vick led me to our room. The moment I stepped inside, my breath caught in my throat. Every inch of the walls was papered with images of Babaji. His face covered the cupboards, the doors, and even the ceiling. The mirrors were no refuge—they, too, were plastered with his pictures, staring back at me from every angle.

While I had always treasured Babaji's presence in my home back in the US, this felt entirely different: suffocating, as though the space had no room left for me, for us, or for anything beyond the guru. The weight of it pressed against my chest, but I pushed the feeling aside. Silently, I placed my belongings in the small cupboard Vick had cleared for me, willing myself to ignore the growing apprehension that had crept in.

As I settled into my new home, I looked for opportunities to fulfill my responsibilities as both a wife and daughter-in-law. Just a few days after our arrival, I learned that two Indian men would be visiting the next morning. They were coming to do some work on the house, but because they were also family friends and followers of our guru, their visit required the highest level of hospitality.

Unsure of exactly how to host these guests properly, I went to the kitchen to see what I could find. I opened the cupboards and began assembling platters and plates, carefully selecting sweet and savory snacks from the pantry to accompany the chai I'd make. I found some joy in arranging fruits and nuts artfully on the dishes, but when it came time to prepare the chai, I hesitated. Chai is more than just a drink; in an Indian household, it is an expression of care, deeply tied to tradition. I knew that getting it wrong might suggest I wasn't capable in my new role, and the pressure weighed on me.

When I couldn't procrastinate any longer, I found the chai masala and added the tea leaves to boiling water. As the steam rose, the sweet fragrance of ginger and cloves filled the air, calming my nerves slightly. I poured the milk slowly, watching as it swirled and blended into the tea, turning a warm, rich brown.

Wheatish, I thought. The perfect coloring of a young Indian bride.

With the chai ready and the table set, I awaited the guests. When they finally arrived, I greeted them with a respectful "Ram Ram," the customary salutation among our guru's followers. "All hail to Ram."

Vick came to the door and greeted them as well. He took on his role as the head of the house and led them to the table.

As I began to serve, I could feel my mother-in-law's eyes on me, sharp and scrutinizing. I didn't need to turn around to know something was wrong. The tension in the room thickened, and before I could gather the courage to speak to her, she had walked away without a word. Her silent departure stung.

What did I do wrong? My chest tightened with confusion and hurt. I thought I had done everything right—*hadn't I?*

My mind raced, replaying every small detail of my actions, searching for the mistake that had caused this reaction. The uncertainty gnawed at me, leaving a tight ball of dread in my stomach.

Vick hurried after his mother, leaving me seated awkwardly in front of our guests—strangers who suddenly seemed even more distant. I forced a smile, my face stiff with the effort, and asked if they needed anything else. The discomfort in the room was undeniable, but it paled in comparison to the suffocating tension brewing within my new family.

After what felt like an eternity, my mother-in-law and Vick finally returned. Her eyes were swollen and red, her lips tight in a frown. She avoided me completely, staring intently at the table. The minutes dragged on in heavy silence until breakfast ended, and Vick led the men to their tasks around the house.

I had just begun clearing the plates when Vick stormed back in, pulling me aside and demanding to know why I hadn't invited his mother to sit with us. The confusion on my face only seemed to fuel his frustration.

It never occurred to me that she would need an invitation in her own home. Blinded as I was by my desperate need for her approval, I didn't realize that I was in a battle for attention, never mind with my mother-in-law.

"How could you not know to do this?" he asked forcefully. "As *sevaks* (servants) of our Sadguru, it is our duty to respect our parents."

I wondered about this. Did "our parents" mean *his* parents? I didn't ask.

Despite the tension I experienced with my own parents, I missed them. I longed to be with them and feel the security of something familiar.

The look on my face must have revealed some of the grief I was feeling.

"You have a duty here, Gangu. You are a woman—you are supposed to know what is needed. This is your home now. Your life is to serve."

I hung my head in bewildered shame, unsure if I could live up to what was being asked of me.

Over the next few days, I tried to feel connected to this new life and my duty. I wanted to find time with Vick. *Perhaps we would understand each other better if we had more time to talk?* I wasn't sure, but I wanted to try. One Saturday, the two of us went to the grocery store, and I decided that this was my chance.

"I really miss my parents," I said, peering cautiously at Vick.

He parked the car and glowered at me. "*My* parents are your parents now. Don't you realize that this is your new life?"

"Yes, I do, and it's all so new. Is it not OK for me to miss my parents?" I ached for him to understand.

"No, it isn't. This is what we have to do to please our Sadguru Bhagawan, and I don't understand why you can't do it." His body was tense, his gaze locked on me with a force that felt almost physical.

I felt my eyes begin to sting, and no matter how hard I tried, I couldn't stop the tears. They spilled down my cheeks, dripping onto my lap as Vick stared at me in disgust.

"I can't believe you," he sneered. He got out of the car and slammed the door.

I was alone again, his words echoing relentlessly in my mind: *"This is what we have to do to please our Sadguru Bhagawan."* But it felt like all the doing was falling on me. What was he sacrificing? What did he have to change?

I felt powerless, as if no matter how hard I tried, I couldn't get it right. The weight of my own inadequacy pressed down on me, convincing me that I was fundamentally flawed—defective in some unfixable way.

***

The shame and helplessness I felt were severe. While I forced my body to move, I often felt immobile. I waited to wake up and realize that I'd had a nightmare, but I never woke. Would this always be how I felt? It had to get better. Perhaps this was what every woman went through after getting married. It's a big change, after all. Perhaps I just needed to give it some time.

I kept going. Cooking, cleaning, respecting. Each morning, I would wake to begin dinner prep, get myself ready, touch my in-laws' feet for blessings, and leave for work. Each evening, I came home to finish dinner, clean the kitchen, do the laundry, sit with the family to watch an Indian serial that told the story of a good daughter-in-law, and go to bed.

One evening, as we finished watching the good daughter-in-law serial, my father-in-law turned the television off.

As he rose from his recliner chair, he looked at me and said, "Gangotri, we are very pleased with you."

At first, I felt relieved. Thank goodness my efforts were paying off. Then, I was confused. What did he mean by that? What were they pleased by? Did the "we" include Vick? My mother-in-law? Were they pleased with my ability to cook and clean or my ability to handle all the drama that had taken place so far? Maybe they were pleased at my ability to shut my true self off and operate as a machine in their service? What was it? They didn't really know who I was . . . unless this really was all that I was.

A little voice inside wanted to scream, *NO! I'm more than this.* And yet, there was another familiar voice, dominant and powerful, that spoke louder and said, *"Be quiet and sit down. If you don't, you will make a complete mess of your life.* At that moment, I knew that my value in this family was conditional.

So, I shut my mouth, sat down, and put on my best "grateful and good daughter-in-law" face. The distress inside of me, however, was mounting, regardless of whether I acknowledged it or not.

***

Within a few months, I landed a job with the National Health Service in London. I was thrilled to start working, but even more than that, I looked forward to having a little time to myself each day. My forty-minute commute became my small window of solitude. Sometimes I'd nap, but mostly I cherished the moments where nothing was asked of me. It felt like a quiet sanctuary, a time that was truly mine.

My salary was significantly higher than anyone else's in the household, and my earnings were deposited into a family account. I was given an allowance of just 100 pounds a month, meant to cover my commute, meals at work, and any personal needs. At the time, I was grateful to have this bit of freedom, small as it was. I clung to it, using it as a reminder of what little autonomy I still had, especially when things felt really tough.

Despite my resolve to mold myself into what Vick and his parents wanted, life had its own way of reminding me that control was an illusion. As Vick and I drove through the bustling city streets to a family gathering, I welcomed the brief escape that being around others would provide—a moment to breathe and reconnect with myself. Yet, even in those fleeting moments, the unexpected had a way of crashing into my carefully constructed façade—literally.

I hadn't fastened my seatbelt, knowing how Vick would interpret it as a lack of faith in his driving and divine protection. Just minutes from our destination, we stopped at a red light. The sudden screeching of tires behind us was the only warning before I was violently hurled forward. A car had crashed into us at full speed.

Vick's instinctive attempt to shield me with his arm was futile. Though the car was totaled, he was unharmed.

In the immediate aftermath, shock and adrenaline numbed my pain, but as the days passed, the impact of the collision set in, and the agony of whiplash became all too real. The initial relief at not being thrown through the windshield quickly gave way to days dominated by intense, nearly debilitating pain. Each movement sent sharp, searing pain radiating through my shoulders and head. I lay on the couch, clutching onto the fragile hope of relief, but the pain forced silent tears to stream down my face. I worried that my family, witnessing me in this vulnerable state, would take my tears as confirmation of my inadequacy. But no matter how hard I tried, I could not hide my anguish.

Gradually, the reality of my situation settled over me like a heavy, unyielding blanket, smothering every ounce of light and air. Inside, I felt hollow—like a fragile shell, a body devoid of its spirit. Each day, as I walked from the train station to my office, a deep numbness enveloped me. I often found myself wondering what it would be like to stand in the middle of the road, waiting for a car or a bus to come and end it all. Would the emptiness I felt now persist even after my body was gone?

Though my imagination frequently transported me to a place of freedom, escaping my marriage felt impossible. I found fleeting solace in daydreams: driving alone, browsing through a bookstore, losing myself in a book, or reconnecting with old girlfriends I hadn't seen in over a year. I yearned for independence that seemed so far out of reach.

About a year after coming to London, during a typical workday, I was on the phone with my mother. I found myself grasping for some sort of light to hold on to. My mother, sensing the despair in my voice, offered words that I clung to then and continue to hold dear.

"When you are living against your nature," she said gently, "it won't last. It has to change."

Her words sparked a fragile flame of hope within me, a lifeline that began to pull me from the abyss of my despair. Their truth coursed through me, sending shivers across my skin as they struck a chord deep within my soul.

Is freedom even possible? What would life be like if I weren't married? The thought was terrifying, yet the alternative felt equally daunting—I feared my strength to endure was slipping away without the possibility of something different, something more.

As I embraced this new sense of aliveness, I found myself pulling away from Vick and his family, unconsciously and instinctively. I stayed late at work and left home early in the mornings, seeking any excuse to minimize my interactions with them. The growing tension gnawed at me, filling me with constant anxiety. I felt perpetually nauseous and watched in dismay as the pounds seemed to melt off my frame.

Concerned, my mom reached out to my uncle and her brother-in-law—"Mausa," as I called him in my culture—sharing her worries. Over the following weeks, my mom and Mausa called me repeatedly at the office, probing about my situation. Finally, they asked me directly if I wanted to leave.

I hesitated. If I left, I'd be violating my loyalty to Babaji. What would people say about him? I had gotten married under *his* blessings. *Wasn't I now obligated to make this work?*

It felt as though my chest had turned to lead, each breath growing tighter as I fumbled for an answer.

What will Babaji think?

"If Babaji wants me to stay, I will. I want him to be OK with it. I don't want my actions to tarnish his name," I said, my voice trembling.

There was a thick silence on the other end of the line. Finally, Mausa spoke. "OK. I'm going to India to see him—I'll ask him then." I could sense the hesitation in his voice and felt relieved that he didn't try to convince me to leave without considering the impact on Babaji.

"Please, let him know I'm committed to following his wishes, whatever they may be!" I pleaded, my voice cracking with emotion.

My greatest fear wasn't remaining trapped in this lifeless marriage; it was losing my guru. How could I possibly exist without him?

Reflecting on it now, the idea of needing someone's permission to live my life seems almost alien. The jail cell I lived in was not just my husband's home. The beliefs I held were terrorizing my life and covertly holding me hostage.

In the months leading up to this, there had been unsettling moments that, in retrospect, were not merely wrong—they were dangerous.

Vick had a way of turning every argument into something life-threatening. Whenever we fought, his anger would twist into something more sinister. "If anything happens to my parents because of you, I'll kill you," he would say, his voice sharp, his eyes unwavering. It wasn't a fleeting outburst. He meant it. And each time, I swallowed my fear, convincing myself that he didn't really mean what he said—that his devotion to his family, or his pain, or his anger, were just overwhelming him.

And then there was his father. I don't even remember what set him off that day. Something had happened—something that had made him angry at both of us—but when he lashed out, his rage had a target, and that target was me. He stormed toward me, stopping just inches from my face, his breath hot, his fury unchecked. "Fucking cunt," he spat, the words landing like a slap.

I stood there, frozen. Not because I was shocked—by then, I had learned that men like him wielded their anger like a weapon, using their words like blows—but because I had nowhere to put it. Nowhere to put the indignity of being reduced to something small and disposable. So, like always, I pushed it down, telling myself to just move forward.

Recalling these moments, the fear within me shifted into an icy stillness. Surrendering to that emptiness felt safer than facing the full weight of my reality.

To my immense relief, Babaji gave Mausa the permission we needed for me to leave my marriage. Yet, even amid this relief, I was overwhelmed by a profound sense of shame.

My mother and Mausa made plans to fly to London. My mother's brother (or "Mama" as I called him in my culture) lived in a town about two hours away. They would stay there as they waited for the time when I would leave Vick's home.

In the weeks that followed, each morning as I left for work, I quietly smuggled away my most cherished belongings—items I didn't want to leave behind. My office became a hidden sanctuary, a place where I stashed diaries, photos, and other personal treasures in drawers and closets.

As time wore on, my anxiety and fear intensified. I stopped eating at home, terrified of what might be hidden in my food. Stories of Indian daughters-in-law being poisoned or worse haunted me, leaving me uncertain of the dangers I faced.

Although they never laid a hand on me, the constant atmosphere of intimidation was suffocating. My mind ran wild with horrifying scenarios, and the combination of fear and nausea caused me to lose twenty pounds without any effort.

As the day of my departure approached, I felt like a hollow shell, my spirit seemingly absent. I grappled with the reality of what it would be like to be free from this marriage. The word "divorced" clung to me like a layer of grime, as if a scarlet letter would now mark me for all to see.

When the morning finally arrived, I gathered the courage to take my passport with me. My hands trembled uncontrollably as I reached for it on the top shelf of the cupboard. What would happen if they discovered my plans? The thought was paralyzing, so I pushed it down as I fled the house in a panic, praying that no one would suspect anything. I exhaled a massive sigh of relief on the train. I vowed never to return to that house without a trusted companion.

Amid the persistent nausea, a flicker of hope began to emerge. Freedom was no longer a distant dream; it was within my grasp. Although the future was uncertain, the chains that had bound me were finally breaking. It was hard to believe, but I was leaving behind a life of entrapment.

That morning, instead of heading to work, I met Mausa and Mama in the city. As we rushed to each other, I sank into their strong, comforting embrace, finally allowing myself to breathe deeply. Their presence was a stark contrast to my own state of turmoil—steady, reassuring, and completely grounded. It was exactly what I needed to feel anchored and supported.

We drove to a friend's house where we met my mother and solidified our plans for the day. Mama and Mausa would drive me to Vick's house while my mother and our friends would follow and wait around the corner, ready to intervene or call for help if necessary. As we turned the corner, I gazed through the windshield of my Mama's car, my heart pounding. I wished with all my might that I could somehow leap forward to a time when this ordeal was behind me.

Terror flooded through my body, my mind racing with relentless "what ifs." My nausea was intense, but there was no turning back now. As I stepped out of the back seat of the silver station wagon, I noticed three pairs of eyes fixed on me from the doorstep. I glanced quickly from Vick to his parents, observing the shifting expressions on their faces—confusion, astonishment, and above all, surprise.

"Come in, come in *Bhai Sahib*," greeted my father-in-law. In our culture, it was customary to refer to other respected men as *Bhai Sahib*, or brother.

"Will you have some chai?" Both Mausa and Mama had met my in-laws at the wedding.

"Not today," Mausa responded. "Actually, we have come to get Gangotri."

"What do you mean? Why? This is her home." my father-in-law replied.

"Well, we think she needs a little break."

"Gangotri, go and get your things, I will wait here," Mausa directed.

Vick puffed out his chest as he stood up. "You aren't going *anywhere*, Gangotri."

Panicked, my body seemed momentarily paralyzed.

My Mama got up to join me. *Thank God,* I thought.

With a look of gratitude toward Mama, I gathered the courage to walk up the stairs with him. He had brought a few big black garbage bags and began to shake them open. Voices downstairs grew louder, and it didn't feel like we had much time.

I opened my cupboards, grabbed what I could, and stuffed it all into the bags. As I came to my jewelry, I looked at Mama to see what he thought.

I thought back to my wedding when, as a part of the ceremonial rituals, my parents had given me 24-karat-gold jewelry sets. There was also a sari and some jewelry given to me by my in-laws.

"Take what we gave you and leave what they gave," he said.

Even though the moment was filled with so much turmoil, his words reminded me of the integrity I had always loved in him.

I crammed as much as I could into those bags, their seams stretched with the weight of my belongings. Mama and I heaved them downstairs, each step proclaiming the reality of our departure.

Suddenly, the sharp sound of crashing glass jolted me. I didn't know exactly what had happened, but I knew we had to leave as quickly as possible. Entering the living room, I saw Vick hurling our wedding picture and other framed photos onto the floor.

With Mama and Mausa by my side, I carefully stepped around the shards of glass, my focus unwaveringly fixed on the door—the only path to our escape.

Vick screamed, "Don't think you can come back after you leave!"

I didn't answer.

My uncles and I struggled out to the car, stuffed my belongings into the trunk, met the other car waiting around the corner, and then drove two hours to Mama's house.

I felt dead inside. Sitting in the car, my body went limp, and I feared I might not make it through the ride. It felt as though my life had come to an end. Despite my yearning for the joy of freedom, I was overwhelmed by a profound sense of emptiness.

Twenty-five years later, as I sit in my office on a beautifully sunny day in northern California sharing this moment, I find it hard to believe that this was ever my life. It feels like a story, someone else's story . . . and yet, it is mine.

7

Wounded

After I left Vick, I spent two more months in England, staying with friends in London to complete my final weeks at work. I experienced a mix of gratitude for my newfound freedom and a heavy sense of dread about my new identity as a divorced woman. Each day, I fluctuated between standing tall and celebrating my independence one moment and feeling vulnerable and anxious, worried that someone might discover my situation in the next moment.

My plan was to return to the US with my parents, who had been living in Saudi Arabia since my father's job had taken them there after my marriage. Their time abroad coincided with the 9/11 attacks on the World Trade Center, and in the months that followed, they felt a shift in the atmosphere—one that made them start to consider leaving Saudi Arabia. When I made the decision to end my marriage and return to the US, it only solidified their choice. They were already thinking about leaving, and the thought of me navigating this transition alone made the decision even easier.

We would all return to Atlanta, Georgia—the place we had called home before I moved to England and my parents moved to Saudi. Atlanta was the most sensible place for us to settle; we had family there, and my parents had stored some of their belongings there before they left.

But before we could begin again in Georgia, I felt the need to see Babaji. Although he had already given me permission to leave my husband, I needed to ask for forgiveness in person. My father agreed to accompany me, so we planned a trip to India.

When we arrived in Babaji's village, I felt like an outsider. Without Vick by my side, I wondered how people would perceive me. A few locals approached, their faces kind yet curious, and soon the questions about him began. I hesitated for a moment, unsure of how to respond. The pause hung in the air, and I caught a flicker of confusion in their expressions.

I adjusted quickly, falling back on the familiar instinct I had honed over the years—reading others' emotions to gauge my place in the moment. If the people around me were at ease, I could be too. If they weren't, it became my unspoken duty to fix it, to ward off rejection or judgment.

With practiced precision, I forced a bright smile onto my face and replied, "He's doing well!" My cheerful tone was a shield, something to defend against their doubts and my own unease, at least for the moment.

Not wanting to draw attention to myself and reflect poorly on Babaji, who had blessed my marriage to Vick, I chose to stay home while my father went to see him. The thought of facing anyone, let alone Babaji, felt overwhelming. I had traveled to see my guru and yet could not summon the courage to step outside in his village.

About an hour after my father left, my phone rang—it was him.

"Babaji is coming to see you!" he spoke fast and purposefully in his excitement.

"I told him you were worried about coming out of the house and he said he is coming to see you, so make sure you are ready. He will be there in ten minutes. I'm coming too."

I was awestruck. *Of course Babaji would be generous and forgiving! That is who he is!*

I quickly tidied up our space and stood by the front door, waiting for his arrival. When the black car pulled up, Babaji stepped out of the passenger seat, his face lighting up with a radiant smile. My heart softened instantly as he climbed the steps toward me. I knelt down, bowing my forehead to the ground at his feet with deep respect. By then, my father had appeared behind him.

Inside, I had prepared a chair draped with a white sheet in one of the bedrooms, a quiet place for him to sit. I led Babaji there, my desire to speak with him alone growing stronger. Once inside, I gently closed the door behind us and sank to the floor at his feet, ready to bare my soul.

"I'm so sorry, Babaji," I said, tears forming in the corners of my eyes.

There was silence for a few moments.

"You did nothing wrong. There is no need for apology." Babaji's words quieted the relentless voice of my inner critic. I gazed up at him, unable to comprehend the grace I was being given. His face radiated pure love, free of any trace of judgment or disappointment, no matter how anxiously I searched for it.

Though his response filled me with gratitude, a part of me still felt unsettled. I couldn't shake the lingering sense of guilt within myself. And yet, continuing to press the issue seemed pointless and almost silly in the face of Babaji's unwavering compassion. I met his eyes, not knowing what to say.

Sensing I was done, Babaji motioned for me to come closer. The flicker in his eyes sent an uneasy ripple through my stomach. Yet, overwhelmed by the immense favor and compassion he had just shown me, I silenced my hesitation and shifted closer to him. Once again, he began to touch me in ways that I had not consented to and did not know how to refuse. I forced my mind to believe that there was something spiritually beyond my comprehension in Babaji forcing himself on me. I felt myself float out of my body and watch the interaction unfold from above. I recognized what I was witnessing, yet it felt too bizarre, too far from what I believed to be true. Confusion clouded my thoughts, but I pushed down the questions pressing at the edges of my mind.

"Be sure to come home tonight to see the family," he said to me on his way out.

I wrestled with the tangled web of thoughts and emotions swirling inside me. I hadn't seen Babaji's family since I left Vick because I didn't want them to think of me as someone who brought shame upon their father's name. Now, Babaji was inviting me to his home to reunite with them—a gesture brimming with kindness and generosity. Yet, the assault just moments before left me feeling disoriented and detached from myself.

Again, I attributed my confusion to my inability to perceive the divine plan behind it all. I convinced myself that there was a greater truth, far beyond what I could comprehend or see.

***

We returned to Atlanta, Georgia, and I spent the first month getting reacquainted with all that I had known and missed. I took the car out and sat at bookstores and coffee shops. I read and explored to figure out what I wanted to do next. I wasn't sure I wanted to remain in the field of healthcare administration, and for a while began studying to take the LSAT, thinking I might apply to law school. I got a job at the local yoga studio and began taking two hot yoga classes each day. It felt good to sweat. After class, I often imagined that I was leaving the damaged parts of myself on the mat and walked out of the studio feeling lighter.

During this period, my parents were grappling with their own challenges. With no source of income and our savings dwindling rapidly, my father began to panic. Despite his efforts to find work, his age made it difficult. They explored various business opportunities, from laundromats and apartment complexes to retail stores, before deciding to purchase a tanning salon. It struck me as odd since none of us had ever used a tanning bed, given our naturally darker complexions.

My mother, however, had a remarkable talent for learning new businesses and selling to customers, even when she had no personal interest in the products. She threw herself into the salon with dedication, managing everything from opening and closing the shop to hiring staff, keeping the books, and maintaining the tanning beds. I watched her with admiration as she studied the lotions and gels used in the process and figured out which products sold best.

While my mother worked tirelessly, my father continued his job search and assisted with the salon as much as he could. My mother excelled at interacting with customers and managing the teenage staff. My father, however, struggled in these areas. About six months into running the business, my mother fell ill, clearly exhausted from the relentless effort.

I observed my parents wrestle with the strain of their situation and their worries about the future. Initially, they declined my offers to help, but I started taking on shifts at the salon one by one. Eventually, it became routine for me to wake up each morning and announce that I was heading to work.

"You are?" my father asked, sounding both surprised and confused.

"Yes, let mom rest at home. I got it."

"You'll have to convince her." He looked doubtful.

"Tell her to call me when she is done with her *puja* (prayers)."

Over the next few months, I took over the daily running of the salon to give my mom a break. When business was slow, I read, recited mantras given to me by Babaji, and researched jobs and schools on the business computer. I found it challenging to relate to our clientele, even though they often saw me as one of them.

"Did you get that tan from these beds?" I was asked on more than one occasion.

I always struggled to know how to respond without sounding rude. "No," I said quietly. "My skin is naturally darker."

These were customers, and as ridiculous as the questions were, I did not want to offend them. They would stare at me blankly after I responded, and I wasn't sure what they were thinking.

Everything I shared with them was based on secondhand information. The idea of laying in one of the tanning beds repulsed me and seemed suffocating. Even just wiping down the beds after each use was enough to make me feel queasy; the thought of actually using one of them was just gross.

While my mom and I were able to manage customers and give them a halfway decent experience, we had no idea how to market ourselves and grow the business. About a year in, we decided to sell. The process took almost three months, and I was relieved when it was over.

After the tanning salon, I knew I needed to find work. Law school sounded great, but the thought of studying for three more years without earning money did not sit well with me. I found a recruiter and began my search. It wasn't long before an organization in New Jersey showed interest in my resume. I was excited to receive their job offer and began making plans for my move. During discussions with my parents, we decided it was time for me to buy a car. Although I was twenty-six, this felt like a significant milestone for me. The idea of having my own vehicle, with the freedom to go wherever I wanted, whenever I wanted, was incredibly freeing.

I chose a Volkswagen Beetle. My father accompanied me to the dealership and successfully negotiated the price to fit our budget. I felt uneasy about the process when the salesman mentioned that he wouldn't even earn a commission from the sale due to the discounted price we were paying.

"They just say that," my father told me. "It's how they sell cars."

I didn't argue. My father told me before we went to the dealership that he would be negotiating hard, and I was to stay out of it. In hindsight, I'm grateful for his advocacy, and I don't know what he could have done differently to help me understand his actions in the moment.

Watching him go back and forth with the salesman made me uncomfortable. The man seemed earnest when he insisted he wasn't making any money on the deal, and I believed him. I felt sorry for him, uneasy about the way this worked. It never would have occurred to me that negotiation was expected, or that his words might not be entirely true. But my father understood the game, even if his approach wasn't always perfect—especially when his voice rose in frustration.

One of the first things I did upon bringing the car home was place a small picture of Babaji on the dashboard. He was my protection, and I wanted him in my car at all times.

The night before my drive to New Jersey, I packed the car with all my belongings, including several framed pictures of Babaji. Each image was carefully cushioned to prevent damage. As I examined the packed Beetle, I marveled at how all my possessions fit into such a small car. Admittedly, the large, 16x20 inch frames of Babaji took up most of the space, so there wasn't much room left for anything else.

It took about a week to find an apartment. I stayed with a friend during this time, and while I enjoyed spending time with her, I could not wait to move into my own place. After signing the lease, I began shopping for furniture and settled on a fresh and breezy bedroom set and a dark olive-green couch and chair with an ottoman. I reveled in the process of setting up my apartment, and when it was finally complete, I cherished my time there. Each morning, waking up in my own space and stepping into my sunlit living room, with the guiding face of my guru on the wall, felt like a true homecoming. I finally had something of my own.

***

During this time, one of my girlfriends, also a follower of Babaji, was struggling to make ends meet. Without a second thought, I handed her my credit card to cover her monthly expenses, trusting she would pay it off each month. Her sister needed transportation for appointments and career-related errands. Since I was just driving to work and back each day, I agreed to letting her use my car.

About two months later, a call from the credit card company caught me off guard. They informed me that my $20,000 limit had been maxed out and suggested I apply for more credit if I needed additional funds. The news hit me like an arctic blast, leaving me momentarily numb.

This isn't happening!

I was just getting back on my own feet and could not believe how shamelessly they had taken advantage of my kindness. When I was able to contain myself, I called my friend and her sister. They argued that they would pay me back but would not commit to a date. Their nonchalant tone confused me. *How is this not a big deal to them?* I told the sister I wanted my car back that day. After more arguing back and forth, she finally agreed.

Over the next few months, I reached out to my friend and her sister several times for the money, but neither ever responded. It was clear that I was on my own, and now my credit was in the toilet.

That fall, I began spending time with a friendly Indian couple from my apartment complex. We grew closer, and eventually they presented me with what they described as a lucrative business opportunity. They introduced me to what I would later learn was a multi-level marketing scheme, enticing me with promises of earnings far exceeding the debt on my credit card—if only I committed fully.

The couple seemed intelligent and sincere, and I struggled to reconcile the possibility that they might be part of a scam. Desperate to fix my financial situation before my parents found out and my credit sank further, I convinced myself that this opportunity was a blessing from Babaji.

I thought back to a few months earlier when I had flown down to Atlanta to see my father in the hospital. He was at risk of a heart attack. I had no idea until my mother called one day while I was at work.

"He's OK, though. He'll be fine," she reassured me.

"Mom, I'm going to come down."

"Why? He's fine! You can't just leave work like that. There is no need for you to come right now." She was adamant.

I was confused. *How is it not necessary for me to be there if my father is in the hospital?* After I hung up the phone, I paused for a moment in my cubicle. I then walked down the hall to my boss's office and told him I would be flying out to see my dad and would let him know when I'd be back.

I informed my mother that I was coming to visit, and thankfully, she didn't argue further. The impact of her intention to not burden me with news of my father's health made me feel distant and insignificant. I couldn't articulate it at the time, but resentment was building within me.

My parents didn't see me as capable of handling anything. I definitely didn't want to reinforce that opinion by letting them know about the financial mess I had gotten myself into.

My ex and I had been separated for almost two years. However, I still hadn't dealt with the trauma I'd been through. I didn't realize it at the time, but I was depressed and looking for distractions and a sense of purpose. This new business seemed like it would be just the thing. I went to a few of the meetings and was impressed by the level of empowerment they seemed to impart to their members, or "business owners." I decided to join and paid the initial $450 to start my business. I worked hard during the day at my job at the hospital and in the evenings traveling and attending meetings. On the weekends, I would spend time with my sponsors to learn the "art of contacting." This involved walking around public places like malls and bookstores and striking up conversations with strangers to interest them in starting businesses under my umbrella. Again, I knew something was not quite right but allowed the speakers at the meetings and the new community I had become a part of to override my instincts. My financial desperation also made it hard for me to see the truth of how I felt.

I racked up even more debt over the next two years as I continued to pay the monthly commitment for my business and develop a shopping addiction, yet another distraction from the void I felt deep within my soul.

Eventually, I turned to another very dear friend and my father for help. While I was deeply grateful for their support, it came with a heavy burden of shame. I couldn't shake the thought that maybe I wasn't capable of managing anything on my own after all.

Despite my faltering confidence, I was determined to find a way forward. I explored different ways to make extra money, and at one point, I began selling Indian clothing out of a rented garage. On weekends, I'd rent a U-Haul, pack it with clothes and racks, and head to local festivals where I'd set up a booth to make sales.

These different pursuits didn't just fill my time; they gave me a sense of purpose during a period when I felt like I had failed everyone around me. They offered a small reprieve from the weight of my pain and the chance to rebuild my life.

8

Dating to Yoga

After all that had transpired over the preceding few years, the idea of marriage felt like a trap. My father, however, was worried.

"You need to find someone and settle down," he would often tell me.

I resented the idea that I *needed* to find someone. *Was I not capable of taking care of myself?*

It was clear that my father didn't think so. While I did not share my dad's opinion, his doubt in my abilities haunted me. My lack of success so far often made me wonder why I thought I could survive on my own. Still sitting in the muck of it all, with lots of debt and not a lot of money, I couldn't see the growth I had been experiencing. I was not afraid of hard work, and I thrived on creativity. The definition of success I was accustomed to was results—focused rather than growth-oriented. This fixed mindset would take years to evolve. Looking back, I wonder what I could have built if I'd had the belief system and frame of mind to do so.

Dad mentioned marriage at least once a week. I was lonely, and though dating seemed daunting, I figured I'd give it a try.

"OK, Dad. I'll get on the 'Indian' dating app each week if you promise to find a hobby and engage with it." I hoped that he would find something other than me to focus his attention on.

"What do you mean, find a hobby?" He sounded slightly irritated.

"Go learn something new. Read a book, play a sport . . . do *something!*" I pleaded.

"Fine," he sighed. "I'll read. And you will look online." An expression of stubborn agreement passed between us.

Though he agreed to do what I asked, it felt like he could only stomach it if he framed it as him giving me instructions. This dynamic was all too familiar, and I was fully aware of the game I was playing. I chose to go along with it.

Is this what it's come to? I wondered as I created a profile on the app. *I have to find a date online.* I cringed. I realize that today it is commonplace to find a date or even a partner online. Back in 2005, however, it still felt foreign to me. I thought back to the times my father had tried to introduce me to men using a "biodata" (a resume for marriage used in traditional Indian matchmaking) he had created.

When I was twenty-one, my father had decided it was time to start looking for a husband for me. Unbeknownst to me, he had written a matrimonial biodata on my behalf and placed an advertisement in the matrimonial section of *India Abroad*, the Indian newspaper.

21-year-old Hindu Punjabi vegetarian girl

Height: 5'5"

Body Structure: Slim

Complexion: Wheatish

Education: Bachelor's degree in mass communications

Sun Sign: Capricorn

Mother Tongue: English and Hindi

Caste: Bania

Mother: Business owner

Father: Chemical engineer

She is very domestic, respectful, and polite, and follows traditional Hindu values.

He had been having conversations with friends and family to "find me a match." Every few days, he would show me pictures of men he was considering.

I could not believe it when he was especially interested in a man who was six years older than me and already bald.

"He is a doctor from a very good family," my father stated plainly.

"What does that even mean?" My eyes narrowed as I examined my father.

"He is well-off, and he comes from a good Indian family with our values," he remarked, as if it were the most basic truth.

"Did you notice his age and lack of hair?" I scoffed.

"Why does that matter? He will be able to take care of you."

I never met the bald doctor, but I did have a few other painful and, in hindsight, amusing meetings with potential husbands.

I met one at a mutual family friend's home. The three families sat stiffly in the living room, the parents doing their best to make the conversation feel casual as they exchanged pleasantries. I stayed mostly silent, and in an attempt to nudge things along, they suggested we take a walk outside to "get to know" each other—as if such a monumental task could be accomplished in ten minutes.

I shot a glance at my dad, my eyes silently pleading for him to step in. Instead, he responded with an encouraging look, deliberately ignoring my unspoken protest. I stayed rooted to my seat, refusing to move. To my dismay, the parents all stood up and went for the walk themselves, leaving me alone with this boy—this man— awkwardly sitting across from me.

He studied me and began to speak. At first, I listened as he told me about his work and family. I began to zone out about three minutes into his monologue. *Does he always talk this much? I really cannot wait to get out of here. I wonder if he can tell how bored I am.*

"So, I think this could work. What do you think?" He peered at me expectantly.

Startled, I stared at him, trying to process his words. When their meaning hit me, I fought hard to suppress my laughter. I hadn't said a single word, and yet this guy had decided we were a good match. *Based on what?*

Though I found the whole exchange absurdly entertaining, a wave of irritation swept over me. Why had my parents insisted on dragging me out to meet him? I had intentionally left my hair unbrushed and wore all black—fully aware of its reputation as inauspicious. And yet, here he was, declaring us compatible. Did he just need a warm body to fill the role?

"Ummm . . . I don't think so. I didn't really want to do this meeting, to be honest." I figured it was only fair to let him know the truth.

He stared at me, his eyes narrowing.

"Oh, I know your type. You'd rather meet in the back seat of someone's car, eh?"

It took me a moment to grasp what he had just said. My eyes widened in disbelief. He really said that. Surely, he isn't *that* rude, I thought to myself.

He continued to stare, waiting for an answer.

"Excuse me?" I asked.

He opened his mouth to speak, but luckily, at that moment, our parents returned. The evening continued with this guy thinking he was flirting with me. During dinner, he tried playing footsie with me under the table. Every so often, he would give me a strange, overly theatrical look—an attempt at seduction that only made me cringe, almost feeling embarrassed for him. After dinner, as everyone settled into the living room to chat, he weaved through the crowd like a man on a mission—just trying to plant himself next to me. I wanted to kick him and ask him if his eyes were malfunctioning because whatever look he was giving me was *not* working. He absolutely disgusted me.

"He was awful. That whole experience was awful! Why did you both leave me with that guy?" I blurted out as soon as the car door shut.

"What happened, Beta?" My father's voice was calm. I had expected an argument to follow my complaints and was caught off guard by his apparent curiosity.

After I collected myself, I decided I would accept my father's invitation to explain. I positioned myself in the middle of the back seat, equidistant from my mother and my father. I thought back to the many car rides and intimate conversations my parents and I had had in this configuration. Perhaps it was the fact that we couldn't look each other in the eyes that made it easier to be vulnerable and feel close to them.

"He was insulting. He said I'd rather meet someone in the back seat of a car." I told them about our conversation and the sliminess I had experienced throughout the evening. They listened, and, thankfully, seemed to be as appalled as I was. After this incident, they backed off, still mentioning marriage frequently, but not pushing specific people my way.

Now, five years after that disastrous introduction, as I filled out my online profile, I appreciated the space and permission to share more about myself and what I was seeking. I made sure to include the fact that I had been married before and that I was looking for a mutually respectful relationship. I wanted to be upfront and honest—no surprises.

The next day, my inbox was full. Most of the inquiries were from men who lived in India. I had been told to be wary of these men as they were often looking for a green card rather than a life partner. Over the next few weeks, I deleted most of the messages. Occasionally I sent out an inquiry to someone who seemed interesting. After a few uncomfortable face-to-face encounters with men I met on this site, I decided I needed a better system to ensure I wasn't putting myself in these situations. I called it the "two weeks strategy." We would speak for at least two weeks before we met in person, and when we did, it would be for coffee. I'd have a friend on standby so that if the meeting wasn't going well, I could shoot her a quick text to stage an emergency call, offering me the perfect exit strategy. I avoided uncomfortable situations using this strategy, and I actually met a few decent people. Though we didn't have the chemistry to date, things stayed refreshingly natural.

One day, as I ate lunch at my desk, I received a message from a guy with an Om symbol on his forehead in his profile picture. *Is that a tattoo?* I was intrigued. I called my office mate over to check him out.

"He's cute!" she teased, giving me a playful look while her eyebrows danced.

I wasn't sure what to think about the Om symbol on his forehead, but his profile lacked the overconfidence and accomplishment gloating I was used to seeing in most South Asian men's profiles. We began to email back and forth, and about a week later, I agreed to a phone call.

He was easy to talk to and clearly interested in me. I valued his well-timed questions and empathy, which set him apart from the other Indian men I had spoken to. He shared openly about himself, and my interest in him grew quickly. After another week of speaking on the phone, we hit the two-week mark and decided it was time to meet. While I normally would not agree to dinner for our first in-person meeting, Sanjay felt different. We settled on a cozy Thai restaurant close to my place, and I shared my address with him so he could come by and pick me up.

I sifted through my closet, looking for the perfect outfit, and selected a crinkly, long black skirt and a red tank. Almost ready, I looked out the window to see if he had arrived. He was walking toward the stairs in a pair of freshly pressed khakis and a printed dress shirt. *Is that how he always dresses?* I wondered. I much preferred a more casual look of jeans and a T-shirt, but I appreciated that he'd made an effort.

The evening passed with ease. I was comfortable around him, and in the next few weeks, Sanjay and I saw each other more and more frequently. Even though we hadn't formally discussed it, it was clear that we were together. My heart did a little flip when I saw him in shorts and a T-shirt. I was relieved not to see the khakis again for a while.

Though we lived about thirty minutes away from each other, we spent most of our weekends together and sometimes even met during the week, depending on schedules. Sanjay loved listening to music and introduced me to his favorite bands. He took me to my first concert, and as I observed the crowd dancing without a hint of self-consciousness, I felt awkwardly rigid. Longing for the freedom I was seeing around me, I made myself move until my body gradually began to loosen up. The smell of alcohol and pot was pungent, but the environment felt lighthearted. I relished the contrast to the strict, disciplined way that I was used to.

Within a few months, we began meeting each other's families. It felt like a natural next step, and the excitement of moving closer to a long-anticipated milestone helped to overshadow the flickers of anxiety I carried within me. Quietly, I worried about how my relationship with his family would unfold, especially given my past experiences.

Sanjay's bond with his mother and sister was unmistakably strong, and I could feel the weight of their importance in his life. His father had passed away when he was just seven, so these relationships held an even deeper significance for him. Determined to foster a sense of belonging, I made a conscious effort to connect with them, burying my fears and focusing on building something meaningful. It felt like a responsibility, but also like a chance to create the kind of connection I deeply craved.

As well as things were going for us, there was one main area that we clashed on. It bothered me because it was the most important thing in my life: Babaji.

"I just don't understand. Why do you need a *guru?*" While there was a hint of concern in his voice, his face was expressionless.

"I can't explain it. The love in his eyes and his teachings connect me to God." Sanjay's face was blank, but I was dreamy-eyed. I paused before adding, "You don't have to believe in him. I just ask that you respect my beliefs and maybe be open to meeting him."

"He sounds like a nice guy. I just don't understand the guru thing. And why do all these people worship him? He sounds like a celebrity."

I could tell Sanjay didn't understand, and as he tried to find answers, he was trying to be as respectful as possible.

"Yeah, he is a bit of a celebrity. People come from all over to see him, and he's often surrounded by famous people." I didn't understand why Babaji's' celebrity status was a problem.

We never resolved the issue. It became something that we spoke about every now and then, and eventually, it seemed that Sanjay accepted Babaji's place in my life.

***

"Pack for four days, and make sure you have your passport," Sanjay told me after dinner one night.

"What? Why? Are we going somewhere?" I was confused.

"I booked a trip to Paris, and we leave in two days."

What? How can I just go to Paris with you? What will my parents think?

I compartmentalized my internal dialogue and allowed only my excitement to show. I had a feeling a proposal was forthcoming. We had been dating for almost a year, and I knew his mother had started to pressure him.

As I packed, I thought about the conversation I needed to have with my parents to let them know I was leaving the country. It was a conversation I dreaded.

"I think you should go." My father surprised me.

Who is this man, and where is my father? How could he be so OK with this?

My mother's response, however, was not so relaxed. "Are you going to have separate rooms?"

I was thirty years old and divorced, and my mother was still asking these questions. Her response did not surprise me, but I was taken aback by my own feelings of anger and resentment at her question. Based on the values I was raised on, her questions were understandable, but there was a part of me that struggled to make sense of them.

She has no idea what it is like to be where I am. She's never been divorced or thirty years old and unmarried. How is it that she thinks she can ask me these questions?

"Sure," I replied flatly.

We arrived in Paris on February 12th, two days before Valentine's Day. We checked into our hotel, an old-fashioned and slightly musty but charming establishment on a side road close to the Champs-Élysées. After unpacking, we decided to explore the city.

Sanjay and I walked to the Seine and got in line for the Bateaux-Mouches, the famous Parisian riverboat. While I had been there before with Vick, it was only now that I noticed the beauty of this city. The crisp, cool air made the sights even more inviting. We boarded the boat and found seats close to the back. Sanjay took my hand as we sat, and the boat began to move. I looked out at the river, marveling at the moment.

"So, where do you want to go for dinner?" I asked, still looking at the scenery.

"Why don't we go here?"

Confused, I turned around to see what he was talking about.

In his hand was an open box with a beautiful ring inside. I stared, my head buzzing.

"What?" My mind tripped over itself as it tried to grasp the conversation we were having and what Sanjay was trying to say. I searched his face, looking for clues to make sense of his words. His eyes were wide with expectation, and his clenched jaw hinted at the tension bubbling beneath the surface.

"Will you marry me?" I could sense his eager anticipation and jittery nerves.

I paused for a moment, gathering my thoughts to answer his question. My lips slowly widened into a bright smile. "Yes!" I beamed.

His face softened as he took the ring out of the box and placed it on my finger. Wrapping his arms around me, he pulled me in for a tight hug.

We enjoyed the rest of the trip, conscious of the extra meaning that had been added to our relationship. Though we had been together for almost a year, the engagement made everything feel new. The night Sanjay proposed, he took me to a small vegan restaurant for dinner. I loved vegan food and was excited to be engaged to someone who knew this about me. The café was down a little side street, and as soon as we walked in, I knew the food was going to be delicious. The air was filled with scents of basil and roasting vegetables as we took a seat by the window with a bottle of red wine. In my excitement and limited experience with alcohol, I only became aware of how much I'd drunk when it was already too late. As I later discovered, I vomited several times that night as Sanjay helped me out of the restaurant.

It was my first and last time getting drunk, but it was a small moment I remember because it signified something so much bigger that was growing within me—an expanding sense of freedom.

***

For the remainder of the trip, we visited the sights, ate lots of food, and enjoyed each other's company.

When we got back to the States, I felt uncertain because I hadn't yet spoken to Babaji about my engagement. I wanted to marry Sanjay, but I wondered how things would be with him not believing in Babaji or even God. I didn't need him to be super devoted because

I already knew what it was like to be married to someone like that, but how would it be to marry someone who didn't believe at all? When we spoke about the issue, it felt as though a small wall of tension stood between us. I decided it was best to avoid this strain and speak to Babaji about it instead.

I set aside time on a Saturday morning to speak to him since calling Babaji took time. There was the difficulty of establishing a clear phone connection, followed by the challenge of reaching Babaji when he was available to talk. It often took a few hours, if not a few days. I was fortunate that morning, and I got through after three or four tries.

"My respects, Babaji!" I trembled as I spoke into the phone.

"Yes, Gangotri. How are you?"

"Good, Babaji. I have something I want to ask you."

"Ask."

"Sanjay asked me to marry him. I'm not sure if I should because he does not believe in you or in God." There was a pause at the other end of the phone line.

"Does he believe in you?" He surprised me with this question.

"Yes, I think so," I replied hesitantly.

"Then it sounds good, child. No marriage is perfect, but if he believes in you, it is a good start." His voice was calm yet strong.

His words brought me a sense of deep gratitude for the care and love that Babaji had for me. It was clear that he had my best interest at heart. Moments like these never allowed any doubt about Babaji to enter my mind. He was so compassionate and did not concern himself with the respect others gave him.

***

Wedding planning was underway, and I envisioned the ceremony taking place at my parents' house in Atlanta, Georgia. Although Sanjay's family lived in California, they graciously agreed to make the trip. This wasn't my first wedding, but it was the first time I felt like I had a voice in how the day would unfold.

After much thought, I carefully selected the garden of an art museum as the venue. My mother had once shared memories of her own wedding, held under the stars at night. Inspired by her story, I stood amid the rose bushes and the serene pond at the center of the garden, imagining a nighttime ceremony illuminated by floating candles.

Planning became a collaborative effort. My father, Sanjay, and I spent a few days taste-testing cakes and catering options, savoring sweets and deciding on the menu. Within weeks, the major logistical pieces fell into place, allowing me to finally see the larger vision coming to life.

Back in New Jersey, Sanjay and I continued with the wedding planning remotely. One day, as I drove to his apartment after work, I called my mother.

"Mom, how are things going with the wedding preparations?" I asked.

"Things are good. Can I ask you a question?"

"Sure."

"When you were in Paris, did you have sex with Sanjay?"

I was stunned. *Why would she ask me this? I'm thirty-one years old and clearly not a virgin.*

"Yes, I did." I stood my ground, my jaw clenched. What else was there to say?

My mother's silence lingered, heavy and laden with everything she wasn't saying. It wrapped around me, amplifying the tension until, finally, she broke it.

"Well, then," she said, her voice calm but firm. "You are on your own for this wedding."

"Fine," I snapped, hanging up the phone with shaking hands.

The frustration bubbled over, leaving me seething as I stared silently at the road ahead.

After all that I had been through, I couldn't believe she was going to pull this righteous bullshit; yet here we were.

Although I knew she and my father would not really leave me to get married on my own, the betrayal of her words cut deep and instilled a sense of doubt. I felt as though the only person I could truly count on in the entire world was Babaji. I had believed that unconditional love was something I could always expect from my mother. That day, I realized just how wrong I was.

The pain of that conversation burrowed deep into my heart, leaving an ache I couldn't shake. After a day or so, I convinced myself to push it aside, thinking I could simply ignore it. What I didn't realize was how profoundly that sting would linger, quietly shaping my relationship with my mother for years to come.

***

Work was going well. Within a few months of returning from Paris, I was recruited by a prominent healthcare think tank in Washington, D.C. It was an opportunity I couldn't refuse and a significant step up from my previous roles. When Sanjay casually talked about moving to Virginia so I could take the job, as though it were the most natural decision in the world, I was smitten.

Because the court doesn't recognize the Hindu wedding ceremony we were planning, we decided to complete our legal marriage before the move. This would not only simplify things logistically but also reassure my parents about us living together.

With the wedding planned for Atlanta, we decided to host an engagement party and courthouse wedding in California, where most of Sanjay's family lived

The engagement party was held at Sanjay's mother's house, and the moment we walked in, we were surrounded by friends and family. The house was packed; the air, festive and warm, filled with laughter and lively conversation. I met so many of his relatives and friends, each of them offering their blessings as they came up to greet us. Sanjay and I sat on the couch like honored guests, receiving well wishes one by one. The night felt celebratory, full of energy, and for the first time, I began to understand just how big of a community I was marrying into.

The next morning, we had our court wedding. Our immediate families joined us as we exchanged vows in a simple ceremony. There were no elaborate decorations or sacred rituals, just the signing of papers, the exchange of words, and the official declaration of marriage. Afterward, we celebrated at Sanjay's favorite Mexican restaurant, enjoying a casual meal together before heading back home. Legally, we were now husband and wife, but it didn't feel complete. The Hindu wedding was still ahead, and until we stood before the sacred fire, I didn't fully feel like we were married.

A week after the celebrations, we made the move to Virginia. I was eager to settle into our new two-bedroom high-rise apartment. One bedroom would be for guests, and the other would be ours. Off the living room, there was a sunroom that Sanjay planned to use as his office since he worked from home.

Shortly after the move, Sanjay left for a business trip. I looked forward to having some time alone in our new space. Setting up our home together had already proven challenging; we struggled to agree on how things should be arranged, and neither of us seemed to know how to communicate our needs without resorting to stubbornness. The tension left me feeling unsure of how to navigate the process, so I decided to wait until he was gone to take charge.

My plan was simple: I would organize everything and make our home feel cozy and inviting in his absence. I hoped that when he returned to a beautifully arranged space, he'd be less inclined to argue about how it had come together.

While Sanjay was away, I took the opportunity to not only organize our space but also handle the mail and stay on top of the bills that arrived. When he returned, he didn't seem to notice the effort I'd put into arranging our home—until he saw that I had paid the bills.

"Why did you do that?" He looked at me, visibly annoyed.

"I just paid the bills," I responded, confused.

"I don't do it that way. I have a system. I'll do it."

Got it. So, I did something wrong since I didn't do it your way?

I did not let him know the volume or strength of my inner voice. It was clear he didn't think I could handle things, and I wasn't allowed to take care of money matters. This is how I interpreted this conversation. Though I was mad, I was used to being told directly and indirectly that I could not handle money and should therefore let someone else (a man) do it for me. I had seen my father express this message to my mother, even though she was often the primary breadwinner in our home. He would frequently refer to the money in our home as his rather than theirs or ours.

"I don't have money to throw away!" he would sometimes say if we wanted something.

Since I was a little girl, I was aware that the money in our home always belonged to the man, regardless of who earned it. I also thought back to the mistakes I had made with my credit card and the debt I had found myself in. I doubted myself even as I felt anger at the situation. *Perhaps Sanjay was right?*

He seemed annoyed for the rest of the evening. I made dinner, and he watched television as we ate. I figured I would wait it out.

Maybe he'll be in a better mood tomorrow.

***

Two months after we moved in together, we flew to Atlanta for our ceremony. It was a busy time, but it was also so much fun to see family who had flown in from all over the world. Everyone contributed to the preparations and various rituals that led up to the big day. It was such a contrast to the first time I had gotten married. I was in my own home and in control of things. Since we had spent months planning, I knew what to expect and was not at the mercy of others.

The wedding was beautiful. The ceremony happened after sunset just as I had wanted, and candlelight made the entire venue glow. I had carefully selected a song that would play as I walked in. It was a Bollywood song that expressed how lucky I felt to be marrying Sanjay. Watching his face as I entered, I don't think he understood the meaning of the song, but he did have a massive smile on his face. It felt like a dream as I walked toward him with everyone we loved there to witness it.

After the ceremony, we were driven back to the hotel where the reception would take place the following night. Sanjay's family had gathered in a large hotel room to formally welcome me into their family. Following tradition, we played a few lighthearted games as a newly married couple. In one, rings were dropped into a platter of milk, and we competed to see who could find them first. Another involved Sanjay untying threaded bracelets my family had secured tightly around my wrists before the ceremony. Laughter and playful teasing filled the room as his family cheered us on.

Soon, the evening came to an end, and I felt a wave of relief. It had been a beautiful but exhausting day, and I was eager to relax and spend some quiet time alone with my husband. When we got to our room, I began getting ready for bed while Sanjay told me he was heading out to see his friends and would be back soon. An hour passed, and he still hadn't returned. Eventually, I fell asleep, only to wake up the next morning and realize he had never come back.

I got dressed and went downstairs to find coffee, wearing the elaborate traditional attire expected for the day after the wedding. It felt strange to dress up without Sanjay by my side, but it was all I had packed for the day. As I wandered the hotel hall, I bumped into a few of Sanjay's cousins. They were sweet and kindly led me to breakfast without judgment. I hadn't seen Sanjay for several hours and assumed he was still out with his friends after a late night of partying. Not wanting to draw attention to his absence, I made excuses when people asked about his whereabouts, hoping he would show up soon.

"I think he's hanging out with his friends since they have come from so far away," I would tell them. They responded with a nod that was both empathetic and inquisitive.

While I wanted him to enjoy himself, I also wanted to be his main focus. We were getting married after all. *I'll be his focus for the rest of our lives,* I consoled myself. *Since his friends had come from so far, it makes sense for him to want to spend more time with them.*

The reception took place that evening, and Sanjay returned to our room to get ready. That night, we let loose on the dance floor, surrounded by family and friends. The music carried us all, blending our laughter and movement into a shared rhythm of pure joy. We danced together, pulling everyone into the fun and creating a celebration that felt alive with energy and connection. It was a night of unforgettable memories and unrestrained happiness. The joy of having so much love crammed into one room made it a little easier to ignore the nagging sensation within me that my relationship with Sanjay was already off to a rocky start.

I didn't press Sanjay about where he was the night of our wedding or why he and I hadn't really connected during those few days. He seemed to be more focused on his friends than on me. I didn't realize it at the time, but once again, I was complying with his behavior out of fear of being abandoned. My mother had already made it clear that she didn't support me. *What would I do if he left me?*

***

We lived in Virginia for about a year after our wedding. It was clear to me that Sanjay wasn't happy there. He hadn't made any local friends and didn't seem to be getting out of the apartment much. The amount of travel required by my work did not give Sanjay and me a lot of time to connect, either.

He began talking about moving to California, and I panicked. Living close to my in-laws was not something I wanted. My last experience with this had been nothing short of horrid, and I was not about to walk into that sort of situation again. I was surprised by his willingness to listen and not push the subject. He suggested that we begin looking for a home in Virginia if we were going to stay there since our rent was so high. I sat with this idea and also began considering a move to California. There was something about Sanjay's willingness to consider my point of view and my fears that allowed me to let my guard down.

Sanjay had a rental property about two and a half hours outside of the Bay Area. If we moved to the golden state, that was where we would live. It would afford us enough distance from his family for us to have our own freedom. After a lot of consideration, I told him I was open to the idea.

"Were you testing me? It seems like you wanted to see if I would stay in Virginia before you agreed to move to California!" He seemed resentful and disgusted.

I didn't know what to say. He wasn't wrong—but why was that so terrible of me? Yes, I did want to know if my feelings mattered to him, and when I first said I didn't want to move, I meant it. I hadn't planned to change my mind if he was willing to stay in Virginia.

A few months later, we moved into Sanjay's rental property in California. It was cozy having our own little place, and I got to know the area quickly. I continued to work for the same Washington, D.C.-based company and continued to travel quite a bit. The demands of my job increased as I worked remotely, and I started to feel overwhelmed and suffocated by the pressure. I developed shooting pains in my abdomen, and when I went to get checked by my doctor, she told me she was putting me on immediate disability.

"What?" I looked at her incredulously.

"If you don't stop and take care of yourself, you are going to end up with a stomach ulcer." She was serious.

"But I have people counting on me. I can't just stop working!"

I couldn't believe this was happening. There was a small part of me that felt relieved that someone was able to see what I was going through, but at the same time, I was terrified of letting my company and co-workers down.

"Take two days and wrap up what you can. You need to take at least a month off," she ordered.

I nodded even as my heart sank.

I drove home with a heavy sense of dread, bracing myself for the conversation with Sanjay. I wanted to call him immediately, to tell him how awful I felt about needing this time off, but I hesitated. I couldn't be sure he would comfort me, encourage me to take care of myself, or understand that this was what I needed.

When I walked into the house, I found him on the couch, watching TV. Without a word, I sank onto the cushion beside him.

"My doctor says I need to take a month off . . . or my stomach could get worse," I said quietly.

"So, you're just going to leave?" Sanjay asked pointedly.

I tried to explain, but he didn't seem to understand.

I wrapped things up at work as well as I could and began my leave of absence. It was hard at first. I felt restless and didn't know what to do with myself. I started seeing a therapist, thinking that perhaps I needed to process my previous marriage a bit more. I couldn't understand why the pressures of my job were too much for me. *Maybe with therapy, I'll be able to tolerate more.* In addition to therapy, I began looking for things to do.

I thought about attending a yoga teacher training program in Hawaii. I hesitated to talk to Sanjay about it. First, I was on disability, and now I wanted to fly to Hawaii to learn to be a yoga teacher? I enjoyed the practice and liked the idea of teaching. It would be such a change from the normal pace of life, and perhaps exactly what I needed. He wasn't thrilled, but he helped me plan my trip.

"When you are living against your nature, it won't last. Life has to change." These words my mother had long ago imparted were once again showing their wisdom to me.

The yoga teacher training pushed me in ways I hadn't expected. The days were grueling—seven to eight hours of hot yoga flow, followed by intense group processing sessions that stretched on for hours. There were moments when I doubted I could make it through, my muscles aching, my mind screaming for rest. I deliberately avoided calling Sanjay in those first few days, afraid that if I heard his voice, I would break down and beg to come home. But by the fourth day, something shifted. A quiet strength settled over me—a realization that I could do this, that everything I needed was already within me. Even as exhaustion threatened to overtake me, I embraced the challenge, feeling more present and alive than I had in a very long time.

When I returned from the training, the world felt fresh and full of opportunity. It seemed as if I had detoxed a lot of the negativity I had been holding on to and could finally see more clearly. I began teaching at a local yoga studio and looking for a full-time job. It took a few months, but I was able to find a position in a large local healthcare organization working on leadership development. Life was starting to feel more settled. Sanjay seemed more content now that I was working, and he was finally in a position that required him to go into the office where he would be interacting with other people throughout the day.

We lived a relatively stable life, and after two years, we welcomed our first child, Arjun. I couldn't understand how I could have so much love for this little human I had just met, and yet I also struggled with motherhood. My strong ideas and lack of flexibility about how I wanted to raise my baby got in the way of precious time I could have had with him as an infant. Wanting to breastfeed a child who for some reason couldn't nurse, I became resolute and committed to pumping for a full year. Rather than spending time with Arjun and feeding him, even if it was formula from a bottle, I spent that time attached to a machine. Doing what I thought was "right" seemed so important that I didn't realize what I was losing.

After Arjun's birth, the thought of returning to work felt jarring and off-kilter. With Sanjay's support, I began to write a business plan to open my own yoga studio. When Arjun was approaching eighteen months, I opened the doors to Veera Yoga. It had been my intention to bring Arjun to work with me. I set up a small cot in the back office with a box full of toys for him to play with. He would have everything he needed there so that I could work and he could be a child. I tried this a few times and soon came to realize it was impossible. Arjun was an adventurous child, full of energy, and the Zen atmosphere the studio required was not a good match for him. In between classes, he would stack the yoga blocks in the middle of the yoga floor and knock them down as he squealed with delight. While I smile as I remember those moments now, at the time, I was torn. Clients came to the studio seeking rest and relaxation, but my energetic toddler was a miniature hurricane. Luckily, despite all of our challenges, my parents—who had moved close to us as soon as they found out I was pregnant—were only too happy to help. This gave me the space I so desperately needed to work.

It took some time to establish my new business, but within two years we were doing well. Evening and weekend classes were full, and I began working on creating a teacher training program to continue to grow the studio. It was clear that we needed to hire more teachers so that I could spend more time with Arjun. Before I could make any progress on that front, another "bump" came along. I was pregnant again. Despite the surprise, I was excited—and so it was that I began the next chapter of my journey.

Part Three

Unearthed

9

Waking Up

It was January 2012. My business was one-and-a-half years old, and I was seven months into my second pregnancy. I stood in the yoga studio bathroom, examining my reflection in the mirror and searching my own eyes for a clue as to what I was feeling. I had just taught a powerful yoga class, guiding my students to reflect on their truth. *Was their practice serving them?*

I looked closely at my brown irises and noticed a sadness I didn't recognize. A whisper rose from somewhere deep within me. *Was my practice serving me?*

Not just the yoga—all of it. My spiritual practice. My devotion. The obedience, discipline, and unwavering trust I poured into him, allowing him to become the deciding factor in every major decision of my life.

My eyes stared back without responding. I waited sensing something just beyond the edge of my awareness. Slowly at first, and then rising with undeniable force, the answer came: a resounding "NO!"

Before I could catch my breath, a tidal wave of truth came crashing in. My practice had never served me. I wasn't even serving the practice. We were both in service to a man who was raping me. And the power he held over me was so complete, so insidious, that he could make me do anything—making me believe all the while that every step was my own choice.

Wait, how could I be thinking this way?

And yet, there was nothing that had ever felt truer. Ever since the day before I married Vick, every time I visited Babaji, he touched me and forced himself on me. Babaji had been using his power to sexually assault and rape me over the last ten years. This truth enveloped my mind, while the faith and convictions I had clung to for the past twenty years struggled to fend it off, resisting its attempt to take root as a new belief. *This can't be true!*

Images of Babaji flashed before me. His compassionate eyes and ways. The security I felt knowing I had him in my life. *What would I do without him?*

I sat with this question as a very stable, grounded, and calm part of me seemed to step outside of the chaos happening within and watch. It saw me having these conflicting thoughts and all the feelings that went with them and yet seemed oddly at peace. This part of me knew that it was time to let go, and it was observing the process of change, the energy of which I had felt when I became pregnant with my daughter. This sense of omnipotence was unfamiliar. I felt my breath flow in a way that can only be described as freedom even as my mind wrestled with this truth.

I thought back to the year before when I had attended one of Babaji's spiritual gatherings. I was in the early stages of my pregnancy—about fifteen weeks along with my daughter. I felt excited to be in his presence while I was carrying her, hoping for his blessings to reach my baby. Yet beneath the excitement, there was an indifference I couldn't quite place at the time. I chalked it up to all the hormonal changes that occur during pregnancy. When I had the opportunity to meet one on one with Babaji, he seemed distant. When I spoke of my pregnancy, he grew even more distant, giving me a blessing that felt more like a brush-off. I noticed this and pushed it aside; I was used to Babaji's changing moods and always thought of them as his way of testing me to see if I was willing to be committed to him unconditionally.

Standing in the yoga studio bathroom, as I processed this new realization, my gaze lowered and caught a slight kick beneath my belly. Placing my hands on my growing bump, I felt my baby's movement—quick and insistent. She was already making her presence known. It was irrefutable: she was here for something important, and she would not tolerate any of this fuckery.

I suddenly felt exhausted. The truth of my situation was indisputable, but the weight of my position felt debilitating.

What have I gotten myself into? How have I been so blind for so long? More importantly, how the hell am I going to get myself out?

Babaji—and all my friends and family tied to him—had been my entire world. *Who would I be without them*? I had begun to taste freedom, but it came laced with a new kind of responsibility: now that I saw more clearly, what would I do with that clarity? What would life look like if I truly disentangled myself from Babaji's orbit? In that moment, the idea of liberation didn't feel expansive—it felt like floating without direction.

Walking out of the bathroom following this immense realization, I felt off balance and needed to sit down.

Everything seemed so surreal. I could not believe that this was my life—AGAIN! The feeling was eerily familiar. When I left Vick, I felt a similar sense of being lost, but there were people in my life who were there to catch me. I wasn't sure if I would have that this time.

For years, I had believed my life would be meaningless without Babaji, and now I was considering deliberately cutting him out of it. My mind wrestled with this truth, but my body whispered something different. Inhabiting my body had unearthed truths I could no longer bury, no matter how fiercely I wanted to. I had been taught that I am not my body. I am a soul, they said, and this body is temporary. While there is truth and power in this teaching, also embedded in it—and in the responses I received from adults when I spoke of the violations I experienced—was a darker message: my body's signals did not matter. I had internalized this so deeply that it had hollowed me out, my awareness slipping from my body like mist dissolving into the air. I drifted through the world like a leaf caught in a current, surrendered to the pull of forces beyond me—untethered, numb, and exposed, open for others to shape as they pleased.

My yoga practice and pregnancy changed that. These experiences demanded that I *feel*—feel things I had long ignored, things I didn't know how to hold. Yoga was not a practice to escape or suppress sensations; it was a place to meet them. The physical signals of pregnancy, I realized, were not just discomforts to endure, but the voice of my growing child asking for care and attention. And so, I began to lean in, to observe. I watched as the tightness, twinges, and shifts in my body spoke to me, asking me to listen—to breathe into what ached and soften into what I resisted. Each breath became a bridge back to myself.

This growing awareness rebuilt a relationship with my body, a fragile trust as though it were saying: "Finally, you are here. Finally, you are listening." The truth of the violations could no longer be silenced because my body now refused to be silenced. I felt this awakening in my bones, deep and unmistakable. And yet, my mind, so accustomed to its defenses, pushed back. It resisted fiercely, clinging to old patterns of disconnection and avoidance. The wisdom of my body, however, once faint, had grown too loud to ignore. And I was finally learning how to listen.

Awake to more than I had ever been, I was still consumed by the fear of not having Babaji in my life. The weight of it sat in my chest, relentless and unshakable for days. About two weeks after the realization in my yoga studio bathroom, I booked a session with a therapist, hoping to make sense of the turmoil within me. In that quiet hour—speaking, pausing, and truly listening to myself—I felt something shift. A spark of courage emerged, faint but certain, giving me the strength to face the change life was asking of me.

After the session, I drove home to my mom, who was taking care of my son.

"I need to speak to you," I told her.

We went into the backyard and sat at the patio table overlooking the pool and fruit trees. The view was tranquil, but my heart and mind swirled like a cyclone.

How do I say this? I wondered. In the end, I opted for frankness.

"Babaji has been sexually assaulting me for the last ten years."

There was a pause.

"What?" my mom asked. Her mouth wrapped around the word as she enunciated it extra forcefully.

"Yeah, he's been raping me for ten years."

"What do you mean?" she asked. "What did he do? And why didn't you tell us?"

I didn't respond. I didn't know how to. There was so much I was processing already. The fact that I had tried to speak up ten years earlier and was shut down didn't even enter my consciousness at that moment.

I searched my mother's face as she sat, deep in contemplation. "I'm not mad at him," she said, her tone measured and reflective.

Immediately, I froze. It was over. I could tell, in that moment, that there was no reason to continue speaking up.

In the years to come, I would look back at this moment for the rage—the searing anger—that I *should* have felt. The kind that I *wish* I'd had. And yet I couldn't seem to find it.

As I struggled through this on my own over the next few weeks, I began taking steps to remove Babaji from my life. I needed to tell my father about the rape and abuse I had endured. Unfortunately, much like my mother, he didn't seem to understand. His reaction left me frozen once again, unable to find the strength or words to explain myself in a way that might truly be heard.

It was becoming painfully clear that I would have to walk this path alone, no matter how much I wished for someone to stand beside me.

About a month after I told my mother, I took down the many pictures of Babaji in my home. I looked through all my old journals and boxes of photographs and removed all remnants of him that I could find. As I thought of what I wanted to do with it all, I knew that the trash can in our backyard was not enough. I did not want his energy anywhere near me, especially as I disposed of it.

While I took these steps, fear began creeping up inside me. I had always thought of Babaji as equivalent to God and therefore extremely powerful. Though I had started to acknowledge his blasphemous ways, I could still feel his power. I felt him watching as I gave him up and removed him from my life. The image of a wild boar with long curved tusks charging at me kept flashing through my mind. I knew that I had to find the right place to dispose of all the things that this demon's energy inhabited.

Finally, it came to me. *The dumpster behind the casino.*

Thankfully, Arjun was at my mother's house and Sanjay was away on business, giving me the space to do what I needed to do. I packed up all the pictures I had just taken down and loaded them into my car. With only six weeks left until my baby's arrival, I refused to let remnants of my abuser linger in my home. I wanted my daughter to enter a space free from his presence, even in the smallest form.

I loaded the last photograph into the trunk and looked around to make sure no one was watching me. I got into the driver's seat, shut the door, and started the ignition, making each small action intentional and deliberate. As I drove the short fifteen-minute journey, I felt an eerie sense of being watched. I had packed all the pictures of this man into my car facing down so that I didn't have to see his eyes. It didn't matter though—they were there, and I couldn't escape them. I took full, deep breaths as I balanced my speed with awareness. Finally, I pulled up behind the building and noticed my hands were shaking.

I got out and walked to the back of my car, glancing around to make sure I was alone. My hands still trembled, and my whole body felt weak. I wasn't sure if I had enough strength to open the trunk. When, finally, the latch released and the trunk opened, books and photographs spilled out onto the ground. Impulsively, I scooped up armfuls of these mementos and began throwing them into the dumpster. I felt a surge of rageful power rising within my body and I used it to thrust the large, framed pictures of my abuser into the casino trash. As I threw the last frame in, it bounced and flew—almost impossibly—out of the trash. This was the large photograph that I had kept on my alter, the one I had worshipped. The glass cracked and shattered across the cement. Hesitantly, I picked up the frame and photo and threw it back into the dumpster. It landed this time.

Shivering, I looked around again to see if anyone was there—if anyone was watching.

I was alone.

I got back into my car and drove home, taking deep breaths all the way. Up to this point, when I felt fear, I called upon Babaji and the mantras he had given me. Now, as I felt this terror, I had nothing to hold on to. I forced myself to remember, *You have everything you need inside of you.* I was determined to cling to this new personal mantra and wondered if I had to fully believe the words for it to work.

As I walked through my front door and stared at the newly empty walls, I felt a sense of liberation that had evaded me for so long. It was as if my body got a little bit lighter and taller. I looked around, searching for something to anchor me. I saw nothing.

Just let it all unfold. I thought. *Trust in yourself, in the divine that you have been chasing. Trust in that.*

It was hard. I wasn't sure how to trust anymore.

I walked into my bathroom and stood in front of the mirror, relieved now that all traces of the demon were gone. I looked at my expanding belly again and thought of the little girl who was growing inside. Once again, I felt the winds of change whispering within. "You have everything you need," she said.

I placed my hands on my belly and whispered back, "The world needs you, little one. Thank you for choosing me to be your mama. I cannot wait to meet you."

***

The next few weeks were a blur. Lost in my own thoughts, I kept circling back to the moment I first met Baba. I had started dropping the respectful "ji" from his name—sometimes even referring to him as the demon he was. The love and gentleness in his eyes, the compassion on his face when he spoke of his own devotion to God— it was dizzying to think about now; the irony was almost unbearable.

While I felt confident in my decision to remove him from my life, there was a tiny voice inside that still harbored doubt. I didn't yet know how to hold on to myself as an anchor.

The actions I needed to take were clear, even though my emotional state was not. Processing it all, I felt alone and vulnerable. In the past, I had always felt as if I could do anything with Baba's blessings. I no longer had that to rely on. I didn't know how to stand on my own or trust myself yet, and the void I felt inside was growing. I began to have nightmares in which the wild boar would charge at me to attack. I knew it was Baba, and, when I was alone, I'd feel those eyes watching me, small goosebumps rising on my skin. When I thought about how to protect myself, I realized that my coping tools were all skills I had learned from him. Where was I to turn?

"Leave me alone! Get out!" I'd scream, squeezing my eyes shut as tightly as possible at times when I was alone and scared.

I began to explore various versions of spirituality and learned about the protection that Archangel Michael provided. As I read descriptions of Saint Michael, his energy seemed similar to that of Shiva from Hinduism. Shiva represents creation, destruction, and protection. Michael's power sounded comparable and gave me comfort. I felt I had found a way to tap into my faith without abandoning myself.

Intense and often conflicting emotions ran through me. I felt hurt, betrayed, and even guilty. How could this man, who was supposed to be my *guru,* do this to me? Had I asked for it? Why didn't I say no?

Amid this rush of feelings, I began to worry about my relationship with my husband. Some of the abuse had happened after we were married. How would Sanjay react to this information? How could I withhold this from him? It was such a huge ordeal in my life, and it had caused so much pain while bringing about so many changes. I feared that keeping this to myself would cause us to become distant. I was changing as a person, and I wanted him to know, but I was terrified to tell him.

So, I waited . . . for two full years.

***

I spent the next several weeks preparing for my daughter's birth. My son, Arjun, really noticed the change when he could no longer fit comfortably in my lap. He would often kiss my belly and say, "Hi, Baby!" to his sister. I loved the feeling that my kids were already connecting.

The birth of my daughter reignited my faith in my own body. My body went into labor without being induced. I celebrated that moment, especially given the contrast with Arjun's birth, which had been so challenging. It was more than just these two experiences being different—*I* was different. My relationship with my body was different, and as a result, my body was responding to me differently. I could finally feel my own physical power.

This little soul that came through my body was a force to be reckoned with. She had her own timeline. When she arrived, three weeks after the doctors expected her, she made it known with her commanding voice.

I remembered the trauma of giving birth to my firstborn. He was also "late," and the pressure from the hospital to induce was substantial. When labor finally began, my water broke, and I thought we were in the clear. As soon as we got to the hospital, however, my contractions stopped. Twenty-four hours later, I was given the induction pill and experienced contractions that were so intense, I wasn't sure I would survive.

On that last day before I went into labor with my daughter, Sanjay and I decided to do a bit of gardening. I ended up filling two large garbage cans with soil as I got our gardening boxes ready for new plants. Just as I scooped the last shovelful of dirt into the container, I began to feel the first pangs of labor.

I paused, a small smile spreading across my face. What my baby girl didn't know was that she was making her arrival into the world in the same way the Goddess Sita had. I remembered the story I had heard so many times in my own childhood.

There was a king by the name of Janak. He and his wife had been wanting a child for a long time. One day at the beginning of the growing season, the king went out to ceremoniously begin plowing the fields. As he plowed, the chisel hit something hard. He stopped and removed the remaining dirt that covered a beautiful chest. When he opened it, he found a beautiful baby girl cooing and gurgling inside. King Janak claimed this child as his daughter and named her Sita as she was born of *Seet* or earth. Sita (or Sia, as she is called affectionately in the village in which she was found) is known across India as a goddess and the model of womanhood.

Sia, I thought. *That will be her name.*

While I didn't realize the truth of it at the time, Sita was also a powerful feminist in her own right.

Sia's birth was the experience I wish upon every woman bringing life into this world. As the contractions mounted, I had surrounded myself with women who reminded me of my own power. With each contraction, I could feel a force rising up in my body. Owning it felt both daunting and necessary to make this experience the sacred threshold through which my daughter would enter the world.

As that force built within me, I could feel Sia's power matching mine and then surpassing it with her determination to be born. As if claiming her victory, she roared upon her arrival, letting us all know she was here to take care of business.

After Sia's birth, adrenaline surged through my body. While my previous birth experience had left me exhausted, this time I felt exalted and wanted to connect with those I loved. My husband, however, was drained from all the support he had provided mentally and physically. He went to sleep while I sat with Sia, admiring her as she nursed and reveling in this powerful new life.

Over the next year, Sia went everywhere with me in her carrier. She taught yoga classes and teacher trainings with me. She was with me at the grocery store, business meetings, and social gatherings. It didn't matter where we were—she was always most comfortable nestled into my chest.

With my daughter always in my arms, I began to realize just how many opinions people had about how a mother raises her children. I got looks of approval from moms with similar parenting philosophies; I saw looks of dismay from those who thought I was spoiling my baby; and then there were those who looked horrified, as if I were suffocating my child. While I felt scrutinized by others, I recognized that I needed to focus on my own values in order to raise my children to be independent thinkers. Gathering opinions from those around me would not get me closer to my "right." This was something I had to look for inside of myself.

***

During the first few months of Sia's life, I marveled at how easy things felt. Sia was exclusively breastfed, so I didn't have to worry about bottles or formula or a pump. It wasn't until she was about six months old that I began to realize something was wrong. She began to throw up after meals, and her skin was covered in a layer of bright red splotches. I would put baby socks on her hands to stop her from scratching herself to the point of bleeding. The doctors advised me to use a cortisone cream on her skin, which—while I was hesitant to do on such new skin—was necessary. Her vomiting, however, continued even as we used the cortisone to soothe the rashes.

I took her to see an allergist, and after doing some testing, her results showed that she was allergic to everything we tested for except blueberries and chocolate. It was hard not to panic. *What was going on with my baby?* Her birth was seamless, and she nursed so easily. This was not supposed to be happening.

I studied the allergy report in detail and began experimenting with foods that had lower numbers than others. I started to notice that when I removed certain foods from her diet, her skin was better, and the vomiting decreased. Many foods—too many—became off limits.

How could a child be allergic to so many things? As I investigated, I learned of a disease called eosinophilic esophagitis (often referred to as EoE), a condition in which certain foods, when consumed, inflame the esophagus, causing coughing, vomiting, and, if bad enough, even choking. I went to Sia's allergist to discuss my findings. He asked me to schedule a meeting without my daughter so that we could talk. I found it odd that he specialized in pediatric allergies and didn't have the patience to deal with kids during an appointment. Despite the warning sign, I scheduled time with the doctor without Sia. During this appointment, I asked him about EoE, and he responded with condescension and disgust.

"Your daughter does not have EoE," he said. "There are very few kiddos with that condition, and your daughter is not one of them. I know that you're worried about her, but don't be irrational. When my kids swell up a bit, I know it will pass. You should relax."

I sat back slightly, feeling a rush of relief flood through me, because the details I had read about this condition and the limited treatments available for it were scary. "So, you're sure she doesn't have EoE?" I asked, completely ignoring the insulting way he'd just spoken to me. In my experience, doctors were good at diagnoses and not so good with communication or emotional intelligence.

"Yes, I'm sure. Your daughter will be fine."

Over the next two and a half years, I trusted this physician's words and waited for her to "outgrow her symptoms," as he'd promised she would. She didn't. I continued to feed her a limited diet, and she still vomited on occasion. In certain seasons, she would vomit more regularly, but since she was continuing to gain weight, I stifled my concerns.

During this time, I visited a chiropractor as my neck and shoulders were sore from carrying my babies around and sleeping with them in contorted positions. Carole, my chiropractor, specialized in women's and children's care. Sia was often with me during my visits, and Carole would ask about her. Over time, I told her about Sia's health issues and the opinions of doctors I'd spoken with. She was skeptical of the advice and lack of treatment we had received. Carole ordered some bloodwork and began doing her own research. After the blood test results came back, she called me.

"Have you heard of a condition called eosinophilic esophagitis?" she asked.

I let out a massive sigh, almost not wanting to know. I had already ruled this out, and now it was back?

"Yes," I said. "I suggested it to the allergist we worked with previously, and he told me I was crazy to think that Sia might have it."

"He said what?" she replied. "Well, it seems like her symptoms and bloodwork match this diagnosis. I think it might be a good idea to get an endoscopy before ruling this out. I don't suggest invasive procedures to patients unless I think they're necessary," she continued. "I believe this is necessary."

Feelings of dread, resistance, relief, and sadness flooded in. While I wanted answers, I did not want *this* to be the answer. I wanted to know that I was doing the best for my child and that having this procedure done was necessary, but I still didn't want to put her through it. I felt as if we were getting closer to answers, and this scared me and calmed me at the same time.

A few weeks later, Sia went into surgery for an endoscopy.

"Well, it looks like EoE," announced our gastroenterologist, as my daughter lay on the tiny bed before us. "She's doing well and should be coming out of anesthesia shortly. We'll send the sample to the lab to be sure, but this looks like a typical case."

Typical? The allergist had said very few children had this condition.

When we met with the doctor for the follow-up and he confirmed the diagnosis, I had processed reality a bit more, and I was ready.

"So, what are our next steps?" I asked.

"We'll get her some medication, and I'll have you speak to our nutritionist."

Medication didn't seem so bad. If it could give my daughter the relief she needed, I was all for it.

But a nutritionist? I was skeptical.

It made no sense to me that the food pyramid that was often touted as the gold standard of nutrition was taught as a one-size-fits-all formula. Previous experience with doctors and their notions about food did not align with my own experience of a healthy diet. I had also learned that physicians do not spend much time on nutrition in medical school. Given their focus on the human body, I couldn't understand why there wasn't more interest in the food that fueled it.

A young man walked into the treatment room where I was waiting.

"Hello, my name is Sam, and I'll be working with you to ensure that your daughter is getting the nutrients she needs to grow."

I smiled and nodded, trying to convey an open and receptive attitude.

"First, we need to get her on a supplemental diet to ensure she's getting enough nutrients and to rule out the triggers for EoE."

"What exactly is a supplemental diet?" I asked.

He handed me a container that looked like baby formula.

"You'll mix this with water and have her drink this several times a day. For the first month or so, this should be all that she consumes."

Despite the shock I was feeling inside, I began to read the ingredients. By the fourth item on the list, my rage was threatening to boil over. Though there was a small part of me that wanted to acquiesce, all I had to do was look at Sia's face to know that it was time for me to stop following and to start trusting my own intuition.

"So, you think corn syrup is going to be good for her?" I asked.

He shuffled his feet a bit, looking uncomfortable.

"This is what we have for this diagnosis," he replied. "It's broken down into a very basic form so that her body can digest it."

I paused, trying to steady myself, but the anger was still simmering. It wasn't full-blown rage, but it was sharp and rising. "Does my daughter look malnourished or like she's failing to thrive?" I snapped.

"No, it doesn't seem that way. This is just the treatment protocol for her condition."

It wasn't his fault; he was doing his best with the information he had. My mama bear instinct had kicked into overdrive, and I tried to soften my approach.

"I think I'll try to figure her diet out on my own. I've been working on it for the past four years, and now that I know she has EoE, I'll be sure to remove the six allergens that cause it, and I'll find nutritional substitutes."

He nodded, told me to follow up if I had questions, and left.

I let out a deep sigh, accepting that I was going to have to do this myself. While I still craved support, I didn't believe it would actually be helpful—it might even make things more difficult. In a way, knowing I would handle it alone brought a slight sense of relief.

We got home, and I told my mother about Sia's diagnosis. She looked concerned and began telling me about the Ayurvedic (an ancient Indian holistic healing modality) remedies she thought might help.

"Mom, I believe in Ayurveda, but without a practitioner evaluating her, I'm not ready to try a bunch of new things. Let's just take this one step at a time and get her some results with this medication. After that, we can look into other things."

She shrugged. While I wasn't surprised at this reaction, it stung. This "I tried but you don't want to listen" shrug always hurt because it sent the message that I didn't really know what I was doing, and I didn't care about what she had to say. It didn't take into consideration what I thought, and my own experience with the situation.

Although I knew I would do whatever it took to keep my daughter healthy, many doubted my maternal intuition. Despite the doubters, I put my head down and plowed forward. Nothing was going to impede my fight for my daughter's health.

I resumed my research to learn more about the latest treatments and assemble the best care team possible for Sia's condition. Over the next two years, I would find several doctors who were committed to getting Sia to optimal health without simply bandaging her symptoms. They weren't afraid to tell me the truth about the hard work it would take.

In time, I would grow increasingly comfortable managing her diet. As the years went by, she became more tolerant of foods and slowly began to manage the condition on her own.

Research on EoE is still evolving, with new information emerging all the time. There is currently no cure for the disease, and the specific allergens that trigger inflammation are not always obvious, making management challenging. Many patients rely on a supplemental diet to control their condition, and I'm grateful that so far, Sia hasn't had to.

Taking care of my daughter and ensuring she was nourished was hard. I was never completely sure if I was making the right choices. Sia, however, seemed to trust that I was. She ate what I gave her and rarely complained about her severely restricted diet. In her own beautiful way, she was showing me how to trust myself and the new boundaries I was creating.

10

Falling Apart

"Where are all the pictures of Babaji?" Sanjay asked.
A few days had passed since that liberating episode behind the casino, and I couldn't hide the fact that the photos were gone.

"I just realized that I want to practice my spirituality in my own way—without following a guru." I shrugged.

Keeping this secret from my husband was suffocating. While my relationship with him was far from perfect, I always strove for closeness and never stopped working on us. But every time I hid my past spiritual abuse and rape from him, it felt like I was shutting off a part of myself, creating a growing chasm I couldn't ignore.

I maintained the façade for about two years after letting go of Baba. Around autumn of 2014, the urge to tell Sanjay became even more intense. I knew that my relationship with him would never feel real if I didn't open up about the rape and assault.

"I have something to tell you," I said. "You aren't going to like it."

"OK," he said calmly. "What is it?"

I paused for what felt like an eternity. At that moment, I was kicking myself for deciding to tell him. My body shook out of fear of what this might mean for me and our marriage. While I wanted to have someone to support me through this, and I desperately wanted that person to be my husband, I also knew that this was not likely. I wasn't sure what he was thinking, but I could tell the prolonged silence made him uneasy.

"I know you have never wanted me to follow Babaji."

"OK." He looked at me, puzzled.

"Well, he sexually assaulted me for many years."

There was another long pause.

Then, he put his arms around me.

"That sucks," he said. "But you know that I'm here and won't let that happen again, right?"

I felt my stomach flip. *That sucks? Is that it?*

Inside the circle of his arms, I remained quiet while I waited. I wanted to melt into him, and at the same time, I hoped that he'd elaborate—that he'd tell me it wasn't my fault, that it had never been my fault. But those words never came.

When we woke up the next morning, he seemed distant. The connection that had been there the night before had vanished. He was cold and emotionless.

"What's wrong?" I asked.

"Nothing," he said, as he went out of his way not to make eye contact.

Deep inside, I knew something had shifted, but I didn't want to believe it. He had been so supportive the night before.

I focused my thoughts. *My hard times are over. It is time to heal now. His mood has nothing to do with me. Perhaps something is going wrong at work. He's never been one to disclose much of how he feels. This must be something unrelated to me.*

After I probed a few more times the next evening, his emotions came bursting out.

"Did this happen after we were married?" he asked.

I was silent. My head dropped in shame as my body trembled. I could feel his stare searing a hole through my soul.

"Yes," I said.

Suddenly, I saw the remote he'd been holding fly across the room, smashing against the wall before crashing to the floor. Plastic shards and batteries scattered everywhere.

"God damn it!" he yelled. "How could you do that? I thought *I* was the most important person to you, but I never was—it was *him*!"

I froze, thoughts and feelings racing through my mind and body. It was so much—too much—and I couldn't decide which feeling or thought to tend to first. There were simply too many to handle at once.

Did he think that it was my fault? That I wanted it and that I enjoyed it? Was this about who was important to me? How *did* I let it happen? *Did* I let it happen? Why do I feel like I *didn't* have control?

It was all so confusing, overwhelming, and shameful.

"I'm sorry. It wasn't like that. You are my husband. He was my guru. I never saw him that way, but I felt I needed to obey him."

I had known this might happen. I needed to give him time to process the news. It was a lot to take in. I had been sitting with it for two years; he just needed time.

"How could you do this?" he repeated.

I had no answer. What he was accusing me of didn't make sense, and yet I felt as if a volcano was erupting all over my life. More than anything, I needed to feel like he was in my corner—that he had my back. Instead, this conflict felt like another weight pressing down on me, unbearable on top of everything I was already carrying. If apologizing and giving him time would allow Sanjay to not be angry with me, then I was willing. I needed him to understand and support me. . . we had to work this out. The whole reason I told him was so he could know all of me—the abuse I had endured and the healing process that was changing me.

I didn't realize it at the time, but the way this played out with my husband was also changing me as I began to relive the trauma over and over again. I doubted my own intentions and questioned my behavior. I began to wonder if I even knew who I was and what I believed. Maybe I didn't know. Maybe I was a completely different person than I thought I was. No, that didn't seem right . . . and yet it did. I was so disoriented.

"Can we go to therapy to figure this out?" I asked.

"I don't know right now." He stormed up the stairs.

Space, he needs space . . . and time, I thought.

✳✳✳

The cold air chilled my bones. Each drop of rain was a dagger stabbing my shoulders as I followed my husband into the therapist's office. I recognized this sensation. It was the same feeling I had before I left my ex. There was little life left inside me, and I moved through the world like the walking dead. I'd often daydream about stepping into the street and being struck by a car. Anything to end this nightmare.

I wasn't sure what to expect in therapy, and I dreaded the thought of having to explain our issue to the therapist. What if she thought I cheated on my husband too? I doubted my ability to withstand both pairs of eyes glaring at me in disgust.

Sanjay and I sat down on opposite ends of the couch.

"What brings you in today?" the therapist asked.

I was silent, hoping that Sanjay would tell her, but he said nothing. The silence stretched on until it became tortuous.

Finally, I began telling her about our life, the sexual and spiritual violence I had endured, and the impact of it on our marriage.

"Our marriage has never been very strong. About two years ago, I realized that I had been sexually and spiritually abused and raped for ten years."

I told her about my religious upbringing and the "guru" I followed for twelve years before he began raping and abusing me for ten years after that.

"I had always thought of what happened as something spiritual or somehow beyond my understanding. I thought of this 'guru' as God and never questioned him." I let her know that Sanjay conflated the abuse I endured with infidelity.

Sanjay sat quietly, tight-lipped.

"So, how do you feel about all of this?" she asked, turning in his direction.

"I don't understand how she could have done this," he breathed, his voice full of heat. "I thought I was the most important person to her, but I was wrong. If he was doing this to her, why would she keep going back to him? It doesn't make any sense."

The therapist listened.

"Do you understand how cults, power, and abuse work?" she asked.

He continued, ignoring the question. "She had *me*! Why did she need to go to this man?" he demanded.

"In a cult, the members are not thinking for themselves. They are under the power of the leader." Looking at me, she said, "I imagine this is not an isolated case?"

"No, it isn't. Others have shared similar experiences with me in the past, and since he's still out there with the power he holds, I assume he probably continues to do this to many other women."

The session went on, and each time Sanjay spoke, I felt myself getting smaller and smaller.

We continued meeting with this therapist for a few sessions with no change in our relationship.

In December, Sanjay headed to India for about four weeks to visit his family. While he was gone, I focused on taking care of myself and my children while staying disconnected from him. I wasn't sure how much time he would need, only that I needed to give it.

When he returned, so did the tension. We spoke only about the kids, and anytime I tried to talk about our marriage or concerns I had, he would respond by letting me know that I no longer had the right to be upset about anything given what Babaji had done, or, as he liked to put it, what *I* had done.

It felt like I was walking on a tightrope, knowing that one misstep could send everything crashing down. Any unhappiness I felt paled in comparison to the weight of "what I had done." When it became too much to bear, I would retreat to a closet or find a secluded spot on the side of the house to release my sobs.

Whether it was my fault or not, he took this situation as a betrayal and was processing it as such. There was nothing I could do to change that.

After another two months, he came to me.

"I'm ready to forgive you," he said.

I felt confused, but knew that if I showed my confusion, it would lead me back to the tension, shame, and grief I had endured over the last five months.

"Really?" I exhaled, feeling so relieved and grateful. "Thank you. Thank you, Sanj."

Thinking back to this moment still makes me sick to my stomach. I didn't know how to listen to my inner voice at the time, and I pushed the confusion I was feeling aside.

Who was *he* to forgive *me*? What was he forgiving me *for*? I hadn't done anything wrong. I was led into an abusive situation by my parents and had followed the lies I had been raised to believe.

At that moment, however, I didn't have the words or knowledge to understand that I was making myself small once again.

Over time, our relationship grew more and more tenuous. We saw several therapists, and each one tried to help my husband grasp what can happen when power dynamics are at play. He struggled to understand and unconsciously held me hostage to his perspective. Each time we had a disagreement, he would think back to how I had (in his perspective) betrayed him. Many times, he referred to the situation, alluding that I had no right to be upset with him for anything given "the guru stuff." The horror of my rape and abuse felt both invisible and enormous during these moments. I didn't yet have the language to respond, but the small flame that had been lit inside me when I made the decision to leave that demon was slowly growing into a fierce inferno of rage. I worried that without a way to deal with my anger, it would burn me alive.

Even though the relationship I had with Sanjay was unhealthy and dysfunctional, it felt like all I had. I held on to it for dear life until it became harder to hold on than it was to let go. I replayed his words in my mind: "I thought I was the most important person to you!" Memories of our wedding night—when he chose to spend time with his friends instead of with me—resurfaced. I thought about the many family gatherings on his side of the family when I was left alone while he partied with his cousins. *Had I ever been the most important person to him?*

We were in the car on our way to get groceries for our family and we began to argue. Grateful that our children were with my mother, I felt my exhales slowing as I awaited the dreaded reference to my supposed infidelity. When it came, I felt paralyzed for a moment, and then, the fire rose. I leaned forward in my seat, turned toward my husband, and screamed, "STOP!"

He was taken aback because I had never responded this way before. "What do you mean?" He looked confused.

"Stop the car, NOW!"

He pulled into a parking lot and brought the car to a halt. I reached for the door handle.

"What are you doing?" he asked.

"I'm leaving. I'm done. I have had enough and will not tolerate you holding my own rape against me!" I looked him in the eyes, surprised by my sense of calm.

"Can we talk?" He seemed softer than he had in a long time.

My sardonic laugh felt like a sword cutting through the bullshit. "It's too late," I replied, as I opened the door and got out.

I began walking, unsure of where I was going. As I crossed the street, I was aware of my husband driving by me. I wondered if he would stop and try to persuade me to get back in the car. There was a part of me that wanted him to—not because I wanted to go back, but because I wanted to reject him once again for all the times he had rejected me. He didn't stop. I kept walking.

About thirty minutes later, my phone rang. I sat down in a nearby bus shelter and took the call from Sanjay's sister.

"He can't keep doing this to you. You both need to decide what you want to do," she said. "I'm not sure you should have told him about this, Gangu."

I felt a bit of relief that at least someone in his family saw what was happening. At the same time, my rage was stoked. *How could I not tell him? I'm not going to live my life in hiding!* If Sanjay and I were going to have a relationship, he would need to not only know about the abuse and assault I endured, but he would have to support me in my healing. I couldn't tell whether he was even capable of that or not.

After I hung up with my sister-in-law, Sanjay called. I sat alone in the bus shelter, staring at his name on my caller ID, uncertain about whether I wanted to answer. Without thinking, almost automatically, my finger pressed the green circle.

"Hello?" I asked, as if I didn't know who was on the other end.

"Hey."

Silence.

"So, what are we going to do?" he asked.

More silence.

"Wanna go to therapy?" he asked.

I paused, wondering how sincere he was. As I gazed down at the concrete, I dragged my foot back and forth against the grain of the cement. The scratching sound it made soothed me. While I could hear him asking about therapy, I wasn't convinced that he was committing to doing the work that would be required to make the process worthwhile.

"We can try," I replied as he pulled up in his SUV. He opened the passenger door and waited for me to get in.

I paused, feeling as though by getting into his car, I was giving all my power away once again. I had doubts about the amount of power I held, but I was very aware of the feeling of loss as I gave in to his wants. I was quiet all the way home.

I knew he loved me and wanted "us" to work, but I was uncertain if we could make that happen. He struggled to see what I had been through as he dealt with the trauma inflicted by his perception of my assault. Our wounds were bumping up against each other, and unless we each dealt with our own pain, we weren't going to be able to have a healthy relationship.

We went back to therapy. Some of it was helpful, and some of it wasn't. I sat on couches with my husband and observed as therapists tried to explain the manipulation and coercion that can happen when someone abuses their power. I tried to stay focused as they told me that my anger was overly controlling and too much for the relationship. Sometimes I stayed quiet, and sometimes the fury inside me came out, seeking a target. No one seemed to recognize my need to be angry. One therapist ignorantly commented, "No one likes an angry black woman." I was stunned and had no idea how to respond. I did, however, know that this therapist needed some training and should not be working with people of color. Needless to say, we never saw him again.

The rage I felt continued to swell, the intensity building into a tidal wave that was becoming harder to hold back.

11

Training

The yoga studio had been open for about five years. I was forty and at a crossroads with my career. The studio was struggling, and although I still enjoyed having it, my passion for teaching had faded. The classes I taught were no longer mine. I had been watching the studios that were always busy and the teachers who packed their students into class like sardines. Having students "mat-to-mat" had become a gauge by which to measure the success of a class. Often, these teachers would create intricate sequences and play popular music. Many students put these charismatic teachers on a pedestal. I remember moments when I experienced a similar energy from my own students. They would come to me with their struggles, asking for advice, and sometimes even tell me that I was their "guru." Hearing this, I would feel a mixture of dignity and disgust.

"I'm not a guru—just a person learning as I go." I would tell them. "When you put me on a pedestal, it's the fastest way for both of us to fall."

Even though there was a part of me that felt a sense of gratification in the respect my students were offering, there was a larger part of me that wanted nothing to do with it. What I wanted was for people to look within, reflect, and recognize that they didn't have to go anywhere to access the wisdom they needed—they already had it.

When I caught myself trying to create classes that mimicked those in the community with the most students, I lost my joy in the art. Imposter syndrome became my dominant mindset, and I dreaded being in front of the room. I had started teaching yoga because of its relationship to my own identity. The root word of *yoga*, "yuj," means to join together. I loved the connection to myself that the practice gave me, and *that* is what I passionately taught. When it became apparent that I was no longer teaching from this place, I realized I needed to stop.

Closing the studio was a big decision, and it took time. I decided to go back to work as a consultant part-time to cover some of our costs while I managed my business. Before the studio, I had been employed in a large healthcare organization coaching leaders across specialties. I had loved this field and checked in with my old boss to see if there were any projects I could take on. The timing was perfect. She needed someone to manage a consortium of coaches the organization was bringing on to support their leaders. I began my role as a consultant, and the stress on our family eased.

I pondered the different aspects of teaching yoga that I had enjoyed. The depth, philosophy, and reflection of the practice were what brought me to life. I remembered the days when I coached leaders. Reflecting back strengths and challenges as my clients shared had been what fueled me. I loved asking questions that encouraged them to explore deeper facets of themselves. Witnessing clients arrive at their own solutions and even healing was a euphoric experience. As I tied this experience to my yoga teaching journey, I decided to get my coaching credential. My boss was very supportive and even offered to cover the cost.

The school I chose wasn't going to be easy. It was a year-long program and cost $10,000.

"10K?" my husband asked. "What will the ROI be on this training? You started the yoga studio and it's not working, and now you want more money to pivot your career yet again?"

"It's being paid for by work," I responded, thinking that would make all the difference in the world.

"It's money that could be used for other things," he retorted.

It felt like a dagger in my chest. I realized that the studio wasn't doing so well, but there had been a time when it was. I struggled to locate my sense of self-worth. Over the past six years, I'd had two kids and an unsuccessful yoga studio.

What is wrong with me? I wondered. *So many women are successful even as they have kids. Why does this feel so hard?*

I didn't respond to Sanjay's hurtful remark. What could I say? I desperately wanted him to encourage me like he had when we opened the studio. I wanted him to tell me that everything was going to be OK. That I was going to be successful. That having two children while owning my own business was not easy. I wanted him to tell me that he was proud of me for trying. I wanted him to be in this with me.

I know now that there was no one in it with him either. The studio was bringing in some money but not enough to cover our expenses. The consulting work I was doing was bringing in a decent amount, but Sanjay often felt the burden of providing for our family alone when the studio wasn't doing as well financially. We were both alone—each of us in our own reality, trying to make ourselves feel worthy while failing to connect with the other. It was painful as we each sought to be OK.

I knew that I needed to do something to make myself successful again. This time, it was going to be a solo effort. I didn't want to depend on anyone. I've realized that the success I pursued wasn't defined by me. I aimed for a "respectable" career, a high income, and a life that appeared well put together. Even now, I struggle to define what success truly means to me. I want to believe it involves fulfillment, happiness, and connection with those I love, but I know that for me, freedom and choice take precedence. Without those, I can't fully appreciate anything else, even when it's right in front of me.

I started my training the following January.

***

In 2016, shortly after completing my coaching credential, and upon the recommendation of a dear friend and mentor, I began training to become a facilitator for the Stanford Graduate School of Business's interpersonal dynamics course. This program focuses on experiential learning through "T-groups," or training groups. During training, we gathered in a circle to practice communicating and sharing feelings and feedback with the intention of cultivating connection and influence. My own feelings often seemed intense, and the permission to share them with others was a gift.

I assessed the group for a few weeks to see if it would be able to handle what was inside of me. About halfway through the training, someone in the group referenced the idea of breaking ancestral patterns. The dam broke, and instantly my eyes became waterfalls. As I tried to hold back, I felt my throat and chest tighten and my body begin to tremble. I wondered what the others were thinking as my heart raced. I was sure they could see my chest rising and falling with each rapid beat. My eyes darted around the room and then back to the floor.

The group facilitator looked at me and gently inquired.

"I really resonated with what you said about breaking toxic generational patterns, as I've been doing a lot of that work for my own lineage. I don't want my daughter to have to deal with the same unhealthy cycles I've dealt with." The words came out choppy and raspy as I tried to overcome the chokehold of emotion I felt.

He acknowledged my disclosure with a nod and a compassionate look.

Another member of the group chimed in.

"I don't want you to feel pressured, but I'd love to know more about your experience."

I paused. This was it. It was a chance to give all that was inside of me a voice. I inhaled deeply and began.

I told them about my childhood and my quest to find a guru to trust and follow. I told them about the abuse and rape I had been through. I shared with them my ongoing struggles with this truth and how these challenges remain very real for me every day.

"So, I very much relate to breaking ancestral patterns. I do it for my children. I don't want them to go through anything like this, and I want them to know their own worth."

The group was silent. I wasn't sure about the nature of the tension in the room. *Had I revealed too much?* I almost didn't care if I had, because the feeling of getting all of this out without anyone questioning my experience was such a relief. I looked around the room and saw many expressions of compassion. I looked for judgment or doubt on their faces and couldn't find it anywhere. I looked down at the floor, wanting someone to say something and wanting to run out of the room at the same time. Finally, someone spoke up.

"Thank you for trusting us with your story," someone said. "I have so much admiration for who you are, that you were able to get out of that situation and then sit here and tell us about it."

I forced a smile. "Thank you."

Acknowledgments and affirmations flew around the room. The response that hit me the most also surprised me:

"I'm so angry at your parents and husband on your behalf," someone said. "They're supposed to protect you and support you, and they failed! I know that they were probably doing the best they could, but I'm still angry!"

No one had ever said anything like this to me before. If anything, the focus was usually on trying to forgive. There was something about this level of empathy that allowed me to exhale fully. I felt seen and heard in a way I hadn't before.

There was so much I wanted to say, but all that came out were tears. It felt as though a pressure valve had been opened, and all the buried feelings were finally free to come out. I locked eyes with group members, silently letting them know how deeply their words had affected me.

The facilitator checked in. "Are you OK to keep going, or would you like the attention to be taken off you for a bit?"

Whew! "Yes, please," I managed to croak. I knew that something immense and transformational had just happened, and I needed some time and space to process it.

The experience of having others hear my story in the way they did was foreign to me. The people in my life were not able to see me or my pain and didn't have the capacity to express the empathy and compassion I so badly needed. When I removed Baba from my life, I also left many of my friends and much of my community behind. I tried having several conversations with loved ones who worshiped Baba. While a few understood and perhaps even respected my reasons for leaving, they didn't believe that it was the right choice for them. Our relationships were not able to withstand my choice and eventually fizzled out.

The loneliness I felt was magnified by the shame that often bubbled up to the surface.

What was my part in this? What if it was my fault? If everyone around me thinks it is my fault, then maybe it is.

These feelings haunted me. Aside from Sanjay—who made it painfully clear that he viewed my abuse as a betrayal—I had no idea what the people around me truly thought. Their silence became its own kind of noise. The unanswered questions echoed in my mind, and in their place, a chorus of self-criticisms rose up to fill the void. They didn't arrive gently—they flooded in, sharp and unforgiving. Why didn't I see it sooner? Was it really abuse if I didn't stop it? Had I invited it somehow? These thoughts weren't rational, but they felt like the only explanations I had. And underlying them all was the question my parents kept circling back to:

"Why didn't I tell anyone?"

Then I remembered. I did. I told my ex-husband, and he had even questioned Baba, whose reaction caused everyone to wonder what I had done to create such an out-of-character response. After that, I hadn't spoken of it until I told my parents and Sanjay.

As I processed the thoughts, emotions, self-loathing, and the breakdown of many of my relationships, I found myself not wanting to interact with others. It felt like too much work. When someone did end up getting a bit close, I worried about having to disclose the horror of my past. It felt like such a huge part of me, and it definitely contributed to how I was showing up in relationships. Trust was hard. I was not yet able to believe that the rape and abuse did not define me; the emotions surrounding it were all-consuming. It was a moment-by-moment battle inside me.

This new experience in T-group showed me that it was possible to experience something different. To be able to be with others as I am felt almost too right. At times I wondered if I deserved such acceptance. After all, these people didn't know me as well as my family did—and yet, they knew much more of my inner world than those closest to me did.

While the conversations within this safe space were deep and meaningful, I found them hard to recreate with people who had not experienced this sort of learning. Slowly, I was able to transfer the skills I practiced in T-group into my life and use them to help build relationships. I was grateful for the language I now had to express emotions and thoughts that previously felt too obscure. The next few years were perhaps harder than the ones preceding them because I now knew what it felt like to belong and to be understood. To know this and not have it in my daily life felt like a cruel trick.

I continued to discover more about myself within these groups at work. Expressing a wide range of emotions was freeing. For example, it was acceptable and even encouraged for me to acknowledge and express my anger in the safety of the group. This wasn't about unleashing it recklessly. It was about finally allowing myself to feel it without shame. Some group members reacted negatively to my anger, while others were drawn in, inspired by the idea that they, too, could access and express their own emotions more honestly. Having a place where I could share this intense feeling and still be accepted gave me hope. Over time, I noticed a shift—I wasn't as easily triggered, and the intensity of my reactions softened. What once sent a surge of heat through my body or made my chest tighten no longer felt as overwhelming. I could feel my emotions without being consumed by them.

The anger I had been expressing in these group meetings, while powerful, had a dangerous quality to it. Those who were put off by it were often reminded of their own traumatic childhood experiences just by the volume and intensity of my voice. I slowly realized that while this powerful emotion need not be avoided, it did need to be tamed. Finding ways to feel it and even express it fully on my own was healthy. In groups, however, modulation was not just healthy, it was necessary for relationships to thrive.

These experiences broadened my perspective, allowing me to finally understand that despite the challenges and the many years they consumed, the lessons learned were invaluable. This small part of my story didn't define me, but the learnings allowed me to define myself in a new way. Perhaps it was this new identity that drew me toward true sisterhood.

In 2020, at the beginning of the COVID-19 pandemic, a dear friend of mine, Mansi, whom I had met through the Stanford program asked if I would like to begin chatting over Zoom with a group of five other Indian women. The only goal of these gatherings was connection. At first, it seemed like it would be just another "to do" on my unending list of things. From the moment we met, however, we felt an immediate connection—our shared experiences, laughter, and unspoken understanding made it clear that we were meant to bond.

Throughout the pandemic, we continued to meet. Eventually, we created a group chat that became a place for us to share our joys, sorrows, frustrations, and anything else we desired. It felt like home. As I shared, I was inevitably supported by another sister. I did my best to show up for them as they shared as well. This group of women was always there when I couldn't find the support I needed in my daily life. They helped me see that I wasn't just OK—I mattered. When reaching out to them with challenges I was facing, they would remind me that I did not need to defend my feelings. They challenged me to look at situations differently and let me know when they saw me taking too much responsibility for situations that were not my fault.

Seeing these women navigate their own struggles was deeply healing for me as well. They were brave enough to ask for help when they needed it, to speak up even when their voices trembled, and to face their own shortcomings with honesty and grace. Watching them lean into discomfort rather than avoid it reinforced for me that vulnerability isn't weakness; it is strength.

These women are all warriors in the way they stand up for what they believe in, and their work reflects this. We embraced both the practical and the spiritual, and one day, in a moment of playful recognition, we named ourselves the Warrior Witches. These women are now some of my dearest friends.

12

My Name Set Me Free

In just a few short years, my world had transformed. I now had the Warrior Witches beside me, and Sanjay, the kids, and I had settled into a new home. Best of all, I had my own office—a room that was entirely mine. It was a sacred space where I could let my creativity flow, focus on my coaching and facilitation business, and most importantly, revel in my own company. In that room, I felt free, unburdened by the expectations or needs of others, and completely in touch with my true self.

Through the window, I gazed at the towering redwoods that stretched beyond our backyard. Their branches mingled with our neighbor's trees, unconcerned with the fence that tried to define boundaries. I couldn't help but reflect on the journey I'd been on— the layers of healing and the parts of my past I had let go of, especially when it came to my experiences with that demon and religion.

But then, as if on cue, a voice from deep within me called for attention.

"You still carry the name."

I was pulled back into the memory, to the moment when Baba gave me the name Gangotri.

The day Baba was set to visit our home in Milwaukee was a momentous occasion, and my family had spent the entire week getting everything ready for him. We deep cleaned every inch of the house, made a variety of sweets, and meticulously arranged the room that had been set aside for him ever since my parents bought the house. Every detail had been considered to accommodate all his preferences. We wanted everything to be just right.

A special chair had been ordered for our living room so that he could sit comfortably while meeting with the many devotees who would come to see him. I decorated the space with flower garlands, vines, and leaves and laid out the crisp white sheets for guests. By the time I finished, the room looked absolutely perfect—clean, calm, and ready for his visit.

When Baba arrived, he took his seat in the special chair we had arranged for him. I felt deeply honored to have him in my home and to be the one fanning him gently. Around 150 followers had crowded into the room, sitting on the floor, their eyes fixed on him in reverence. As I waved the peacock feather fan rhythmically, I glanced out at the sea of faces, all filled with awe.

After about thirty minutes, Baba looked over at me and signaled that he would like to go upstairs to freshen up. I nodded, and as he stood, he pressed his hands together in a gesture to signal that visiting time was over. Like the parting of the red sea, the crowd created a clear path for him to walk through. All eyes followed him as he moved toward the stairs, with smiles and admiration lighting up their faces.

My father and I followed behind as we showed Baba to his room. After taking some time to freshen up, he returned and sat in the rocking chair we had prepared for him. I sat by his feet, looking up at him, and he smiled down at me, his gaze warm and gentle.

"Gangotri," he said as if offering me a gift.

I looked up at him. "What?"

"Gangotri—your name," he explained.

I must have looked shocked at the weight of the name because he then said, "If you don't want it, you don't have to take it."

"No, no! I want it!" I blurted.

I had asked Babaji for a name. Who was I to reject it?

We had visited Gangotri, the sacred source of the Ganges River, just the year before. The place was stunning, and I experienced something deeply peaceful and spiritual while I was there. The river flows from an immense glacier, also called Gangotri, and carrying that name felt as weighty as the glacier itself. It wasn't just a name—it felt like a responsibility, though I wasn't entirely sure what I was meant to uphold.

The peace I had felt in Gangotri stayed with me, but the name itself grew heavy, as if I were carrying part of that glacier within me. Over the next twenty-five years, while carrying this name, I was repeatedly violated by this demon, and I embarked on a long journey of self-discovery. I began to understand my own spirit, my truth, and my place in the world, until eventually, the weight of the name became too much to bear.

It was time to find a name on my own terms. I could feel the importance of this next step toward healing. I had gone from Nirmal to Gangotri. From unblemished purity to a sacred and unmoving glacier. They were both so enormously heavy, and as I held both of those names, I bore all that weight on my soul. I was ready to put down the burden and find some levity.

I thought about changing my name, but I had no idea what my new name would be. I didn't want to simply search for names online or find a name that I wouldn't need a phonetic explanation for every time I introduced myself.

I thought back to 2014 when I felt a strong urge to remove the tattooed signatures of that demon from my arms. Since I couldn't completely erase them, I decided to transform them into meaningful images that reflected my own power. I chose to transform one tattoo into a tree of life, symbolizing my embodiment of motherhood. On the other arm, I created a symbol of femininity, honoring my strength and creative essence.

Unlike the tattoos, where I felt clearly inspired to transform them into symbols of my own power, changing my name felt far more complex. I didn't yet know what name would feel true, and I didn't want to choose one just for the sake of having something different. I wasn't looking for a name that sounded easy or required less explanation—I was looking for a name that would feel like mine. So I waited, trusting that when the time was right, the right name would find me, just as I was beginning to find myself.

****

In 2022, shortly after beginning to write this book, my father told me that my cousin's son was getting married in New Delhi, and I should consider going. My first reaction was an immediate "Hell no!" Going to India felt disturbing given all the mixed feelings I had toward my culture.

I thought about it over the next week, however, and considered what it might be like to visit my motherland. I reflected on what I might want from a visit to India, and it didn't take long to figure out. I wanted to visit my maternal grandmother, my Nani.

My Nani and her baby died during childbirth when my mother was a little over a year old. After she passed, my mother was incredibly heartbroken and confused. She would wander from room to room, crying for her mother. Her family was not able to tolerate her grief and decided that it would be best for my grandfather to remarry so that my mother could have a maternal figure in her life. After finding a new match for my grandfather, his family destroyed all of my Nani's pictures and belongings, thinking this would be in the best interest of the family moving forward.

Neither my mother nor I have ever seen a picture of my Nani. Though she was effectively erased from the family's memory, I have always felt her presence nearby.

In 2020, during the COVID-19 pandemic, my husband, kids, and I were living with my parents while our home was being built. Perhaps it was this proximity to my mother that brought about a desire to connect with my grandmother in a deeper way. I thought of her often and imagined what she might have been like. In my morning meditation, I would feel her watching over me.

As I reflected on my identity and the significance of my name, I couldn't help but wonder how much of who I truly am comes from me and how much has been passed down through my maternal lineage. What beliefs, values, and perspectives were inherited from generations before me? And how could I even begin to distinguish between what is mine and what is theirs?

These questions felt critical, as I believed they held the key to my own freedom. How could I fully embrace my sovereignty without knowing what truly belonged to me? I often pondered these thoughts with the Warrior Witches, who grappled with similar dilemmas. It was the only space where I felt free enough to explore these deep uncertainties. I can't recall how it started, but at one point, several of them began sharing their experiences with plant medicine as a path toward discovering their own truths. I listened with curiosity, longing for a way to connect with my own essence but also feeling uneasy about the intense journeys they described. Over time, as I listened to more of their stories, I realized I needed to experience it myself. Eventually, I gathered the courage to commit. Sanjay agreed to accompany me to a weekend Ayahuasca ceremony, where we would take part in two nights of ritual and exploration.

The first night was overwhelming as the medicine began to take hold of my body, leaving me feeling vulnerable and out of control. Even after the formal ceremony ended, I was deeply moved by the guides, or *Curanderos*, as they are called. They stayed by my side, singing *icaros*—sacred medicine songs—and supporting me gently through the completion of my journey. Their unwavering care, even in my most helpless state, was nothing short of awe-inspiring.

On the second night, I struggled once again to surrender to the experience. One of the Curanderos, sensing my inner turmoil, led me outside, knowing intuitively that the trees and the stars would guide me. As she slowly walked away, the soft jingle of her necklace caught my attention. I was inexplicably drawn to the sound, and even as she moved further away, the sweet ringing grew louder, as if it were coming toward me. In that moment, I realized it wasn't her necklace at all, but the sound of my Nani's anklets. A flood of excitement and disbelief washed over me. She felt youthful and full of joy, and I was overcome with a longing to see her face.

"Show me your face, Nani!" I exclaimed. "Show me your face!" I could sense her presence deep within me, but I was filled with an overwhelming desire to actually *see* her. I felt like a child as I bobbed up and down in my chair with excitement, almost unable to contain myself.

I felt her take my hands to my own face. "Your face is my face," she said. "Your hair is my hair."

I began to kiss my own hair and felt myself trying to find a way to kiss my own face as well.

She giggled as I sat with her, trying to take in all that I could.

"Nani, what would you like to call me?" I asked.

"You are the playful one," she lovingly replied.

I wasn't sure what she meant and remember giving her a side-eyed glance.

She smirked.

"What do you mean?" I asked.

"Your name is Chanchal."

"Chanchal? I don't like it!" I declared and then proceeded to stick my tongue out at her.

She giggled again and said, "See? I told you!"

I couldn't deny it. I *felt* Chanchal.

In that moment, I felt a split deep within me. One part of me wholeheartedly embraced the new name, ready to embody its energy, while another part resisted, uncertain and hesitant. The Chanchal side of me, always playful and mischievous, stood back, watching this inner struggle, and found it all amusing. Every time the resisting part questioned how I could possibly live up to such a wild name, or recoiled in fear of the change, Chanchal would burst into laughter. The feeling was so contagious, I could feel joy bubbling up inside me, and I couldn't stop giggling through the rest of the ceremony, as if I was in on the joke with her.

After the weekend, I was giddy with excitement over my new name.

I began looking up the meaning and discovered that in addition to playful, it also meant unstable, the wind, and chaotic. I looked out the window of my office into my backyard as I sat with these meanings and realized the name was perfect.

There is an instability in chaos; however, there is also a force and a knowing in the wind. I could see it as I watched the breeze meander through the trees. It was purposeful, beautiful, and untamed. This description reminded me of Kali Ma, a goddess in Hindu mythology. She is the embodiment of ferocity, chaos, compassion, and destruction.

When I relate the name back to myself, I can feel the ways in which I have never been OK with the way things are. Shaking things up and challenging norms is one of the things I do best. There is a voice inside of me that doesn't accept the idea that this is just how things are. When something doesn't resonate, this voice will get louder and louder until I listen. Chaos and upheaval are often the by-products of this process.

My name gathered more and more life as I began to make it known to others. While some people joyfully embraced my new identity, others felt threatened by it. Many of those closest to me struggled to understand or respect my decision to change my name, often making it about them rather than me. I couldn't comprehend how my name—a deeply personal choice—would impact anyone else. Yes, there would be a transition period. People would need time to adjust and get in the habit of using my new name. It would require a willingness to honor my wishes. But beyond that, I couldn't see why this decision should matter so much to others.

What irritated me most were the people who felt they should have a say in what my new name would be and others who believed I shouldn't change it at all. While I've always known that people have opinions about everything, even things that don't concern them, it was still surprising—and frustrating—to witness their resistance. This aversion to my name only strengthened my resolve to fully embrace who I am.

Recognizing that it might be exhausting to continue having these conversations on my own, I decided to bring the topic into the open in a way that couldn't be ignored. I made large stickers with my new name and placed them on items I frequently carried—my computer, water bottle, phone, and so on. I updated my name on social media and began signing emails as "Chanchal (formerly Gangotri)."

It worked. People began approaching me to ask about my new name. While some were still resistant, this strategy helped me take control of the narrative and get the word out. It felt liberating to own my identity and share it on my terms.

The excitement and power I felt when I first received my name from my grandmother fluctuated. There were moments when I questioned whether I should change my name and times when it felt simply exhausting. I reflected back to when that demon changed my name to Gangotri and how people responded. Everyone was overjoyed, and people respected me for giving my power to this "guru." Now, as I try to reclaim my identity and assert my name, the process is grueling. The patriarchy is a well-oiled machine. I have felt it trying to chip away at me little by little so that I would give up. I was grateful for my awareness of what it takes to go against the grain. It reminded me of what is needed to be true to myself.

I remembered my grandmother and her erasure following her death. In taking my new name and standing in my own identity, I felt myself standing for her, my Nani. It was worth the strife, the exhaustion, and the pain. The connection was and still is palpable. In standing for her, I stand for me, and as I stand for me, I stand for her.

Sitting here in my office, writing this book and reflecting on my role both personally and professionally, I find that the name fits. I tend to stir things up, and although this has often made me feel like an outcast, my new name makes me feel like I am embracing a gift that I can be proud of. I can finally be me, and my name has had a huge role in setting me free.

13

Motherland

I looked out the oval window, saw the lights down below, and realized my plane was approaching the New Delhi airport. It had been sixteen years since I'd last seen this city. I remembered the strong wave of heat that would hit my body upon exiting the plane. *What will it be like? Does it still smell like a mixture of incense, animals, sewage, and tropical flowers?* In the end, I realized it didn't matter. I wasn't there to see the sights of my homeland. I was there for only one reason: my grandmother. My *Nani.*

***

Over the years, I've been curious about my Nani, occasionally asking questions and wondering about the slim chance of a photo of her still existing somewhere. Since 2020, however, I have felt her presence around me more viscerally. She enters my thoughts regularly, and there is a way in which I feel her with me, watching over me and wanting to connect with me. I have welcomed her company, as she feels like the mother who was lost inside of my own—the piece my mother needed to be able to mother me.

I love my mother dearly, and she has shown up for me in ways that many daughters can only dream of. All that I have been able to do and experience post-children is because of her willingness and ability to care for my kids. Motherhood is exhausting, to say the least. Some of the ease I have experienced is because of her.

While my mom has been there for me in these ways, in many other respects, she has not. I have always felt things deeply, so much so that I cannot dismiss my emotions. They will often gnaw at me until I pay attention. They are paths that must be followed to gain the wisdom they are intent on imparting. My mother struggled to understand this, and at times I felt dismissed and judged as overly emotional, sensitive, and weak. While I know that her conscious intentions and heart have always been in support of me, there have been times when the words that left her lips have caused years of heartache.

As I've connected more deeply with my Nani, I've started to reflect on my mother's difficulty being with challenging emotions. When grief, sadness, or disappointment arise, she often rushes to cover them up—sometimes with forced optimism, sometimes through distraction, and sometimes by skipping straight to lofty spiritual ideals, as if the messiness of human emotion can—or should—be transcended. It's like she's trying to leap over the pain rather than sitting with it. I've felt that in my own life too—her urge to fix, to move on, to smooth things over instead of holding space for what I was feeling. Not having the support or space to grieve her own mother, I wonder where all those feelings went.

While my Nani could not be there physically, I feel her so strongly in the emotional realm—always present. In this way, emotions are deeply spiritual for me—not distractions to be managed, but messengers pointing me inward. They've been a powerful pathway to my own divinity, helping me connect with something greater than myself through the truth of what I feel.

That connection—the emotional and the spiritual—brought me closer to her than I ever expected. But it also awakened something physical, something tangible: a longing to meet our family in person, to walk through the home she lived in, to be held by the space that once held her.

When my father asked if I would come with him to attend a family wedding in India in November 2022, it took me a while to decide. Despite my desire to reconnect with my Nani's family and land, the idea of going there terrified me. Ever since I ended my relationship with Baba ten years earlier, I had gone through many variations of disgust with my culture and country. It is a place where the feminine is touted as sacred but the reality of how she is treated is the opposite. These feelings were very real and important to experience, but I also felt an intensifying yearning to restore my connection and reclaim my heritage, beliefs, and culture on my own terms.

I looked at my father and said, "I will come with you on one condition."

"What is that?" He looked amused.

"You will take me to Punjab to meet Nani's family and see the house she lived in."

"We can do that. We just need your mom to contact them and make arrangements." Dad seemed pleased.

My parents had just come back from a three-month trip to India. Before they left, I asked my mother to meet her family and try to find a picture of her mother. While she was able to meet with members of her family and spend time with two of her mother's sisters, she was still not able to find a picture. The connections she built, however, paved the way for me to visit my Nani's family and be on the land she lived on.

Pulling out my suitcase to pack made the anticipation for my upcoming trip feel a bit more real. I'm not sure what I was expecting, but I knew that I was experiencing a turn toward my own sovereignty. As I faced all that had suppressed and oppressed me over the last decade, I felt exuberant. I finally had the chance to own what was mine and leave the rest behind. Going back to India as Chanchal felt like vindication. A growing sense of the energy that only the steadfast truth brings began to swell inside of me.

Embodying my new name, I could feel the connection to my entire maternal lineage behind me, pushing me forward to reclaim what had always been mine. When I landed in Delhi, there was a familiarity that was undeniable, despite how much things had changed. The last time I was there, the roads were gravel and unfinished and the air was a bit clearer. This new version of ancient, with its flyover roads and parking garages, felt both quaint and intimate. I saw my father waiting for me as I walked out of the airport doors. The smoky smell was both worrisome and comforting. It reminded me of the smell of a *havan*, a Hindu fire ritual.

Dad hugged me, and we walked toward a large man who was the driver of the SUV my father had rented. He led us to the third floor of the parking garage and loaded my luggage into the trunk of his car. My father and I got into the back seat, and our driver began our journey toward Punjab, where I would be meeting my extended family. As I looked outside, things were both familiar and strange. The rickshaws and three-wheelers mixed in with so many cars. People were weaving in and out of traffic, begging for money, trying to get to work, or taking their children to school. The roads looked well-kept and were not as polluted with garbage as I remembered.

The buildings were run down, and signs for businesses were everywhere.

A familiar sense of belonging and reverence cautiously tiptoed into my awareness. When I was younger, these feelings would pounce on me the moment I arrived in this country. Now, they were hesitant to show themselves, and as a result, I felt some numbness . . . perhaps from the anxiety of being there and the memories I had of this nation, or perhaps because I had too many expectations of how I would feel beforehand. As we drove, I noticed billboards with pictures of my abuser advertising his spiritual gatherings. Seeing this monster, I felt sick to my stomach as I thought about how he is still out there, likely manipulating and taking advantage of other girls and women. While I wanted to do something about it, I knew that going down that path would take a lot from me, and there are other things important to women's sovereignty that I feel more equipped to do.

I pondered this as we approached Ludhiana, the city where many of my Nani's relatives live. I felt some excitement rising, and my heart beat a little faster knowing that I was so close to others who knew her.

What will it be like to meet them? What will I say? Will they be excited to meet me? Will they feel our connection is as important as I do?

Dad and I settled into our hotel, and I texted my aunt to let her know we were here. We decided to meet the following evening.

When we arrived at her home, the servant, Ramu, answered the door and led us to a sitting room in the main area of the home. The decor featured rich and regal tones of purple and red. The Victorian furniture and the beautiful marble floors felt almost museum-like. While there were touches of India as well (the temple area and the pictures of gods and goddesses adorning the walls), it was fascinating how much of this home was foreign. Ramu brought us water, and while I wanted to gratefully accept it without asking for anything more, I knew we needed bottled water. For those not accustomed to living in India, drinking tap or even some filtered water can lead to dysentery and other intestinal issues. I hesitated but explained our need, and Ramu readily complied.

His ease in fulfilling the request made me reflect on the tension I felt—the discomfort of asking for what I needed versus his willingness to provide it without a second thought. Deep down, I longed to fully immerse myself in my Nani's world, to eat what they ate, to drink what they drank, and to share in their way of life without hesitation or barriers.

Slowly, members of the family began to trickle in, introducing themselves. There were several distant cousins, second aunts, and uncles along with their spouses. In Indian culture, while lineage is important, we don't typically distinguish between first, second or third degrees of relation. Family is family, and the strength of a bond is shaped more by the closeness we build than by technical labels.

I had so many questions, and yet I held back, not wanting to seem overly eager or intense. After we got past some small talk, I asked about my Nani. Did anyone know anything about her? Since she died seventy years ago, I didn't think anyone in the room would have known her. As they thought about it, they realized that since she was the oldest sibling and they were all children of younger siblings, they didn't remember her. They did, however, recall my great-grandmother, Dwarka Devi, and began telling me about her. She was strict as she had ten children to care for—five daughters and five sons. She lost the power of her voice from shock when my Nani passed away at such a young age. My aunts and uncles described her condition, saying that she would gather all her words and let them all out at once because it was hard for her to speak with a normal cadence.

The evening went on, and we learned about each other as we ate. The food was delicious and seemed to be never-ending. While these fried delicacies are not my normal indulgences, they helped me to feel connected to my culture in my family's home. Soon, it was time to go. I was to meet with another aunt and her mother—my Nani's youngest and only living sister—the next day. Several of my relatives said that they would try to meet me again at that time. We left with big hugs, and my heart filled with love and a new sense of belonging.

The next day, when we arrived at my aunt's home, again we were greeted by a servant who led us to a sitting room. Soon, after drinks and food arrived, my Nani's youngest sister, Lata Masi, walked in. She was short and had my mother's cheeks. Her age made it hard for me to read her face, though I desperately searched for evidence that she was happy to see me. I stood up and she came, took my hand, and sat down, motioning for me to sit with her.

"You've come?" she exclaimed.

"Yes Masi, I wanted to see you!"

"After all these years."

"Yes," I said.

We sat holding each other's hands in silence. I knew then that she *was* happy to see me, and it felt surreal to be there with her. Soon, my aunt and her husband came and sat with us. We engaged in the normal formalities, and then I looked at Masi.

"Please, tell me about my Nani!" I begged.

"I remember her well," Lata Masi mused. "I was the youngest, but I still remember. . . She was very pretty."

"What did she like to do? What did she like to eat? What was her favorite color?" I asked.

"In those days, we didn't have preferences," Masi said. "We took what we got, and we were happy."

Yes, how would anyone know what my Nani's preferences were? She was a woman in India in the 1940s!

I wondered if the answer would be the same if she had been a man.

"I was always the wild one," Masi told me. "I used to dress in style, and I remember once, I got a *parandi.*" A parandi is a women's hair ornament made of multicolored silk threads and decorated with an ornamental tassel. "Pushpa (Nani) loved it and one day, your Nana (grandfather) asked her to wear one."

"Pushpa asked me for mine to wear, and I didn't let her wear it. I still regret that to this day. I had no idea that she had such little time left," Masi said mournfully.

I listened intently as Masi looked at me.

"Your profile looks just like hers!" she exclaimed as she cradled my face in her hands.

I was elated. Nani had told me that I looked like her during the Ayahuasca ceremony. To hear this again from her sister touched me deeply.

"Can I tell you something, Masi?"

She looked at me expectantly.

"Nani came to me, and she gave me a new name."

"She came to you?" she asked. "Really?"

"Yes. She named me Chanchal," I said, feeling both nervous and excited. I wasn't sure how she would respond to this or if she would believe me. I so badly wanted her to share my joy.

"That's wonderful!" said Masi. "I'm Chanchal too." she added with a smirk. "I've always been the prankster and the playful one."

I felt an even deeper kinship with her as she took pride in these qualities.

Masi asked for a picture together, so I gave my phone to my aunt. Masi put her hand on my heart and instructed her daughter to ensure that the picture captured her gesture.

At that moment, it felt as if Nani had come to me in the form of Masi's hand on my heart. It was as if the bond that had always been there between us was becoming visible, and it was beautiful. It was visceral, and yet I wondered if I was dreaming. While her expression remained relatively unchanged, the love that poured into me from her hand was electric.

Over the next two days, I had the opportunity to spend lots of time with my family. In between these visits, I went out into the city to do some shopping. While I rarely wear ethnic clothing back home, it felt comforting to be surrounded by it. I bought a few items for my children and myself. As I shopped, I wanted to experience comfort in wearing traditional clothing on a regular basis.

Maybe I'll try to integrate some of these items into my regular wardrobe. I thought back to my high school years when I had tried to incorporate tunics and shawls into my daily wear. It was an odd feeling to want to wear traditional clothing but not have it be perceived as such. The desire to belong to both my motherland and the land I lived in was both strong and hard to fulfill, given the stark differences in cultures.

My aunts gave me a few shawls, and I imagined wearing them back home. They felt like a quiet reminder that my lineage is always with me and a way to keep my heritage woven close.

I knew that I would miss everyone I had met when we left Ludhiana, and I was also looking forward to our next stop in Ambala, where my Nani had lived in the early 1950s. My aunt had contacted her brother who lives there and asked him if he would take me to my Nani's old home. I was touched at his enthusiasm to meet me for the first time and show me this place that felt so sacred to me.

When we arrived, we had to park quite a distance away because the narrow roads would not accommodate the size of our car. We walked through the small, crowded streets and alleyways to get to his home. Shopkeepers sat on small stools within their roadside stalls, watching as we walked by. I could tell from their stares that they knew we were not local. The roads were uneven, and every twenty steps or so, we would walk around a pile of cow dung. As chaotic as it was, it felt familiar and even a bit like home. The smile on my face as I walked was so different from the perma-smile I often wore in situations where I wasn't quite sure how or if I fit in. I felt a deep sense of connection and comfort, a feeling that this was—and still is—home.

After my father and I greeting my uncle, his son (my cousin), and his family, my uncle looked at me and told me how much I resemble my mother. As he spoke, he had tears in his eyes, and I could tell that there was much more he wanted to say.

"I'm so glad you came" is what came out.

"I've been wanting to meet you all for so long, Mamaji!" I replied. It was a name reserved for my mother's brother.

"You want to see the house they all lived in, right?" my cousin interrupted.

"Yes, the house my Nani lived in!" I replied.

"Let's go there first, and then we can come back and chat," he said. "It's about a ten-minute walk from here"

We began walking through what seemed like the same narrow streets we walked through to get to my uncle's home. The city of Ambala is very old, and as I looked up, I was taken aback by the historical architecture and carvings. While the other places we visited on this trip seemed more contemporary, I found the antiquity of this city to be beautiful and felt myself falling in love with it.

"Do you visit this home often?" I asked my cousin.

"We never come here," he replied. "You have come all this way to see this home, and we live here and never visit it."

I thought about this and how I take for granted the things in my own life that are easy to access.

"I don't think the entire house is still standing as it was sold and is being demolished," my cousin told me.

I took a deep breath. *Thank goodness I'm here to be able to see something!* I thought.

When we arrived, we stopped in the middle of one of those extremely narrow streets and in front of a shopkeeper sitting in his stall.

"This is it," my cousin said, motioning to the opposite side of the street.

As I looked toward where he was pointing, I saw a massive set of double doors with an Om carved into the wall above them. They were beautifully ornate with a reddish golden tint. On either side of the doors was a shelf that had the grandiosity of an altar. On one of them was a large red candle holder. While the beauty of the entrance to this home was apparent, it was also clear that it had not been tended to in years. There was wire around the door handles, cow dung on the steps to the entrance, and peeling paint. There were rocks and bamboo sticks littered everywhere. People passing by stopped and looked at us, wondering what we were so enamored with as we stared at these two doors. I didn't care.

"This is the only thing left of the home. Everything behind these doors is being demolished," my cousin announced.

As I looked up at this majestic entrance, I felt as if I were being taken back in time. I imagined my Nani and her brothers and sisters going in and out of this home. I pictured the inside of the house and imagined a large central courtyard where the children would run and play. Looking up from this courtyard, I could see three floors of the home with hallways circling the courtyard, beneath an open ceiling where the moon and stars would be visible at night. I felt the hustle and bustle of the household that several generations had inhabited.

"It's beautiful," I said, as I came back to reality.

My cousin nodded. "It hasn't been cared for in years."

"But I can tell that it was gorgeous!" I replied.

"Yes, it was."

I stood there staring at the entrance for a few more minutes, not wanting this moment to end and trying to figure out how I might extract even more from this experience. I didn't want to miss a thing.

My dad looked at me. "Shall we go?"

I nodded, knowing that it was time even though I didn't want it to be.

After taking several pictures, we began walking back toward my cousin's home.

We ate a delicious lunch prepared by my cousin's wife of dahl (lentils), roti (an Indian flatbread), and sabzi (vegetable stir-fry). When we were finished, I pulled out the family tree I had started. My cousin studied it carefully, helping me to fill in the names I was unsure of.

"Do you know where there might be a photo of my Nani?" I asked.

He turned, picking up some photo albums. "There must be a photo somewhere!" he agreed.

I was excited because this was the first time I had heard anyone sound confident that we might be able to find a photograph of my Nani.

He had many of the family photo albums, and as we talked about them, he realized that the photos in these albums were all taken after Nani's death.

"There are a few more albums I need to find. When I do, I will look for pictures of Nani and get them to you," he said.

I was grateful that he sounded so committed to helping me get these photos.

"Thank you."

"There is no need to thank me. You have come all this way. It is the least we can do," he replied.

Our next destination after Ambala was Haridwar. As we traveled, I found myself reflecting on the days when I had planned this trip. My father had been adamant about visiting this sacred city along the banks of the Ganges River—Gangaji, as she is affectionately known—a river deeply revered in Hinduism.

The Ganges originates from several sources, but one of the most significant is Gangotri, a massive glacier in the Himalayas. At the time, I was in the process of shedding this name, and I felt a quiet resistance to anything connected to it. However, as I considered my father's strong desire to visit Haridwar, I realized that returning to this city, and more importantly, to Gangaji herself, was something I needed to do.

As a child, I had a deep love for Gangaji and remember visiting Haridwar and bathing in the fast-flowing river. The city has always been bustling with vendors selling bangles, *Kumkum* (red powder used to honor deities), purses, idols, and other articles for ritual and worship. The uneven cobblestone streets were crowded with shoppers and pilgrims traveling to and from Gangaji. Some of these pilgrims were barefoot, wanting to ensure that they did not pollute the path to this sacred river with their shoes; some were nomads carrying all their belongings on their backs; and some were families wanting to share the experience with generations older and younger. The air was crisp, cool, and filled with scents from fire ceremonies, fried food, and flowers that were being sold in the market as offerings for the river. Many of the streets were closed to vehicles and filled with pedestrians.

We arrived around 10 p.m. and checked in to our hotel. The next morning, my father and I set out for Gangaji, walking through the crowded streets, dodging street vendors, cows, and dogs. As we approached Har ki Paudi (the stairs of God), one of the most sacred *ghats* in the city, we stopped to turn our shoes in at a stall for safe keeping. Shoes are not allowed close to the river and are often stolen by the monkeys if left unattended. We proceeded toward the current, and as we got closer, I felt a twinge of excitement bubbling up inside. My father began walking fast and kept looking behind at me with an expression that said, "Hurry up!" I paused and asked him to slow down.

"I really want to absorb this experience, Dad. It's been a long time since I've been here."

"I understand that." He nodded as he slowed down a bit.

The *ghat* was huge, and there were temples on the ground and in the trees. There was so much to see that I would occasionally stop just to take a moment to soak it up. I felt a surge of energy, as if I were coming home and discovering it for the very first time. I had been to this exact place many times before, but I felt as if I were a different person standing there now—so, in some ways, it was an entirely new experience. I saw things as they impacted me, not as I thought they "should" impact me. I was focused on my own experience rather than worrying about what I was supposed to feel.

When we got to the edge of the river, there were chains and ropes attached to the stairs that descended into the water. Bathers held on to these cables to avoid getting swept away by the rush of the river. There were several families bathing nearby. Sounds of joy and laughter filled the air as they named their family members each time they dunked themselves into the water. I stood on the banks with my feet in the river, watching them for a bit.

"Go on," encouraged my father. "Get in!"

"I will, in my own time," I replied.

I tuned my father out and focused on my own experience. Gangaji was cold as she swirled around my feet, beckoning and daring me to come in farther. As I did, shivers raced up my spine, and at the same time, I felt a warmth fill my chest and belly. I knew this feeling. It was as if Mother Ganga was welcoming me into her arms as only a mother can. Submerging my body in the river, I felt my grandmother and all the women before her with me, holding me, supporting me, letting me know that I am loved. I began to cry tears of relief as I allowed myself to be held in this way. I looked out at the expanse of Gangaji and felt a sense of awe and wonder that was both familiar and new.

I'm home, came a whisper.

***

Our trip to Haridwar was short. After bathing that morning, we packed up and left for our next stop in Meerut. It was about a two-and-a-half-hour drive, which was the perfect amount of time for me to sit and process the experience I had just had with Gangaji. I was glad my father wasn't very talkative as it allowed me to be alone with my thoughts and feelings even as I sat next to him in the car.

When we arrived in Meerut, we were met by my husband's aunt and uncle. They had been waiting and greeted us with wholehearted hugs. We went inside, and I noticed that the normal awkwardness that I had felt at other homes when we first arrived was not there. Sanjay's Chachaji (a name given to a father's younger brother) was so jovial and filled the air with so much love that there was no room for awkwardness to settle in. I immediately felt connected and at home. As I sat there, looking down at the table full of snacks and chai that Chachiji (Chachaji's wife) had brought out, I mused at the incongruity of this relationship, as I remembered many other interactions with in-laws that were not so effortless.

Dad and I sat and talked with Chachaji and Chachiji about their son and the house renovations they had done over the last few years. I told them about my new name, hesitantly wondering if this would be the thing that would create distance between us. I was delighted when they listened lovingly and withheld any judgment. My thoughts went to my Nani, thinking about how proud and happy she would be to see her granddaughter standing for her in front of her in-laws while still being loved and accepted. I felt a warmth over my shoulders and knew she was there absorbing it all.

Our final stop was New Delhi for my nephew's wedding. I was eager to reconnect with my cousin brother and his family—it had been over twenty years since I'd last seen him. As an only child, I considered my cousins to be my siblings. Over the years, he would call occasionally, expressing his wish to stay in touch more often.

When I was younger, I used to send letters and *rakhis* to my cousins every year. In India, Raksha Bandhan, a holiday celebrated in August, symbolizes the bond between siblings. On this day, a sister ties a decorative string around her brother's wrist as a token of protection, and in return, the brother gives her money or gifts. As time went on and life became busier, I stopped sending those letters and rakhis. Gradually, we drifted apart, losing the regular connection we once shared.

Now, I've reimagined Raksha Bandhan in a way that feels meaningful for my own family. Both my son and daughter tie rakhis on each other, exchanging gifts as symbols of their mutual affection. It's heartwarming to watch them adapt this tradition to fit their relationship, adding their own unique touches. Last year, Sia gave Arjun a dragon costume—a gift that was far more thoughtful than it first seemed. Her older brother is always asking her for hugs, which she often resists. But with the dragon costume, she made a sweet compromise, telling him that whenever he wore it, he could hug her, and she would accept. It wasn't just a gift; it was her way of showing love on her own terms, creating a bond that is uniquely theirs.

Approaching Delhi, I could smell the smokiness in the air. I reminded my father to put on his mask as his lungs tend to be sensitive. When we arrived, we entered my cousin's three-bedroom high-rise flat, and my cousin brother's wife, Bhabhi as I call her in my culture, greeted us. The space was cluttered with items for the wedding. We sat down, and soon my cousin came out and I was introduced to my niece and nephew for the first time. Over dinner, we had intermittent conversation about how our trip had been so far and what was to come in the days ahead as we prepared for the wedding. While I wanted to connect with my niece and nephew, they were quiet and answered my questions with single words or head nods. After dinner, we agreed to be back the next morning at 8 a.m.

The next few days were interspersed with ceremonies and preparations. My Bhabhi hired a few more (than usual) servants to come and help. One of them, Renu, was there to focus on beauty treatments and massages to help my Bhabhi get through the wedding. She has some health issues that made it hard for her to stand for long periods of time. When Renu arrived, she was joyful and chatty as she gave my Bhabhi her mani-pedi. As the days went by, however, Renu's face began to fall. She was being asked to do so much more than what she had come to do without any sort of explanation. She was expected to work in the kitchen, run out to get last minute groceries, clean, serve guests who arrived, and so on. With each passing day, I noticed that the servants were treated more and more like robots and less and less like people. My connection with this family began to diminish as I tried to check in with the servant staff to see if I could help. The few conversations I had with the help felt more authentic than those I was having with my relatives. As additional family members arrived, my disdain only deepened.

One of the ceremonies included a traditional greeting for the Mama (the mother's brother). When my Bhabhi's brother and his family arrived, we gathered at the door to honor and welcome them. Following custom, the sister was expected to wash her brother's feet to cleanse the fatigue of his journey. As this was being discussed, a young servant girl entered the room carrying a basin of water for the ritual. I waited, expecting my Bhabhi to step forward, but instead, she instructed the servant girl to perform the washing. I was stunned—not because my Bhabhi chose not to do it herself, but because she preserved this outdated custom by handing it off to a young servant girl whose role—and perhaps livelihood—depended on her compliance. I stood there, dumbfounded, trying to fathom how I would endure the next few days without speaking up.

As the days went on, I couldn't ignore the way these servant girls were treated. My mama bear instincts flared, wanting them to have the courage to use their voices, to say no. But I knew the truth: their lives had left little room for "no." They had been raised to tolerate, adjust, and be endlessly flexible—qualities celebrated in Indian women but ignored when dignity and boundaries were at stake.

I also understood the harsh reality they faced. Any defiance on their part could carry consequences far beyond a scolding—a tarnished reputation, a loss of income, or even dismissal. In a system where their humanity was often overlooked, speaking up wasn't just difficult—it was dangerous. People would do whatever was needed to protect their own standing, especially if the harm landed on someone society didn't truly see. The weight of it all felt too familiar, striking uncomfortably close to home as someone raised with similar beliefs about "service." At the same time, I was acutely aware of my privilege in comparison—aware of how easily I could name the injustice while these women had no choice but to survive it.

Indian weddings are full of festivities, food, and celebration. The whiplash I felt from witnessing various levels of oppression to getting my *mehndi* (henna) done and dancing with my relatives around the horse that carried my nephew into the wedding venue had me feeling unsettled and disoriented. I felt gaslit as I experienced the guilt of not being overjoyed that my nephew was getting married. No one around me seemed to notice the disparities that slapped me in the face every time I saw them.

I sat with my Bhabhi's sisters at the *mandap*, or wedding canopy, watching the ceremony. The gazebo under which it was held was beautifully decorated with colorful flowers. The swishing of Indian apparel in bright colors with gold, silver, and sparkles made the entire scene look as though it was straight out of a Bollywood movie. Next to the mandap was a buffet of appetizers with almost any fruit you could imagine, savory dishes from all over India, and sweets that were as colorful as the rainbow. The air was cool, and the gentle breeze was just strong enough to create ripples in the chiffon material so many of us wore.

Occasionally, I would be asked to play my role in the ceremony as the groom's Bua (sister of the father). I would tie the bride and groom's scarves together, signifying their new bond, and placed a lovely sari over the head of the bride signifying that she was now a part of our lineage. The symbolism was deep and beautiful. When the occasional oppressive pieces of the ritual came up such as giving the daughter away as a gift or donation—*kanyadhan* as it's called—it felt as though I were being jolted awake from a pleasant dream. Sitting with the family, I overheard a conversation among my

Bhabhi's sisters about plans for the new bride, who would arrive home that night.

As elders from the bride's mother-in-law's side of the family, they assumed the right to dictate what would happen on the couple's wedding night.

"In our home, when the bride comes for the first night, she sleeps with the Saas (mother-in-law)," one of the sisters said.

"Yes, yes, that is the custom," another replied.

I was stunned.

What in the world does that achieve, other than reinforcing the mother-in-law's control over the new bride?

Traditionally, in Indian weddings and married life, the groom's side holds more power than the bride's, and within that, certain roles are weighted more than others. My Bhabhi—my brother's wife—was the groom's mother, but I was the cousin sister of the groom's father, which gave me, in this twisted hierarchy, a little more power. Her sisters technically had no formal standing in the new household, and yet here they were, setting rules for the bride as if they had some authority to do so.

I decided to use the power this custom gave me—unearned though it was—for something that actually mattered.

I looked at the sisters and my Bhabhi.

"In our home, we don't do that," I announced firmly.

Then I turned to my Bhabhi and met her eyes. "You know what happens in our home," I said, reminding her how we had welcomed her, years ago—how she had been led straight to her husband's room with dignity and warmth, not tested or controlled.

There was a surprised silence.

I surmised that it was because the youngest woman had just spoken up to challenge the elders. The fact that I was from their sister's husband's family seemed to create a bit of a bind for them, and while I could see the tiniest bit of hesitation in their eyes, they resisted.

I got up and walked around the gazebo toward my cousin brother, the father of the groom, who was sitting on the floor witnessing the wedding.

I whispered in his ear, "Why are you letting them force the new bride to sleep with Bhabhi?"

He looked at me, a bit puzzled.

I repeated myself, standing firm, "Why does the new bride have to sleep with Bhabhi tonight? This isn't right!"

"The *pandit* (priest) has said that today is not an auspicious day for them to consummate the marriage," he replied calmly.

"Why did you ask the *pandit*?" At every step, I found myself even more shocked. I could not believe that he had asked the priest about his son and daughter-in-law consummating their marriage!

"Well, now the *pandit* has spoken, and if we do not follow his advice, we will worry about something bad happening. Better to follow his advice." My cousin replied, seeming completely rational.

I was appalled at my family's lack of ability to take responsibility for and trust their own decisions and actions.

The *pandit*, my Bhabhi's sisters, my Bhabhi, my cousin brother, all of them . . . I couldn't believe it.

There had not been any progress made in India—at least not on my father's side of the family. All the progress was surface level—the flyover roads, the malls, the homes . . . the progress was toward capitalism. Patriarchal values had not been questioned, reflection had not happened, and we were still stuck in ancient times. I could not wait to leave.

***

Two days after the wedding, it was finally time for me to return home. I felt relieved and, at the same time, dreaded the flight time it would take to get back to California. My stomach was starting to feel uneasy, letting me know that I had eaten something or had something to drink that did not sit well in my body. The thought of a five-hour plane ride to Singapore and then a sixteen-hour flight to San Francisco was daunting. With the new (to me, as I had not traveled to India in sixteen years) airline baggage rules that only allowed for one checked bag, I needed to either pay for the extra bag or pay for an upgrade that would include the allowance of an extra bag. I upgraded and immediately dreaded my husband's reaction when he found out.

While I earned money, the judgment over how it was spent was hard to bear. As a young girl, I remember looking forward to the freedom that adulthood would offer me. Looking at my life now, I realized that I still had not hit the age where I was experiencing freedom—and I was forty-seven years old. I had been told that earning money was important because it gave us choices. That "us" didn't seem to include me. The choices were for the men of the family to make. I was to contribute to the earning and benefit from the choices *he* made. I could not, however, make those choices myself.

As I sat with these thoughts, I felt a churning in my belly. I couldn't tell if this was due to the unsettled stomach I had from eating something my body did not like, or if it was the churning of change. Either way, I knew that I needed to own my choices and my freedom because no one was going to hand it to me. I felt empowered and selfish at the same time. I had done enough work on myself to know that the selfish feeling was not mine. It was left over from generations of women giving all of themselves to others and leaving nothing for themselves. It was time to change this for me, for my daughter *AND* my son, and for the generations to come. It was time to include ourselves in the "we" that we shaped our lives around. I felt both sick and empowered. This was not going to be easy.

As I walked through the door of our home, my husband greeted me with a detached hug.

"Hey," he said with a smile.

Our connection felt extremely thin.

And then he said, "You spent three hundred and fifty dollars on an upgrade?" His face was expressionless, concealing something much darker beneath.

There it was. It felt like a knife to my belly. His words and expression left no room for any sort of connection.

"Is this what we do now? The next time I fly, I'll just go first class." His tone seemed normal, but his words were cutting.

I was so happy to be back in my own environment, and then there was this—the shaming for not following the rules that he thought "we" made but really *he* made.

I looked at him and walked away, not wanting to get into it.

My thoughts were racing, and sensation overwhelmed me— almost as though the ground were caving in underneath me. My entire body trembled, and I wondered if I was feeling regret about my trip. It wasn't a feeling I was familiar with. The drastic change between Delhi and California was staggering. My husband's reaction added to it at a time when I just wanted to be held. For several days, I felt restless, tender, teary eyed, and unsure of what I was experiencing. The vulnerability of my state allowed old thought patterns to resurface.

Maybe I shouldn't have done that. I just messed everything up. I could have come home to a welcoming husband, but then I had to go and mess it up just for the sake of comfort. How selfish can I be?

Finally, I messaged the Warrior Witches.

"I feel that every time I get back from India," Sheila said. "Right now, you have to take care of you. Don't worry about Sanjay or anyone else. Take the time you need to get back in touch with yourself. Then you can figure everything else out."

I let out a huge sigh of relief. My sisters had my back at a time when I couldn't bolster myself.

"You didn't do anything wrong. It's not like you spent thousands of dollars. It was a minor upgrade."

They commented as if it was the most obvious thing.

Sigh . . . I remembered the choice I had longed for all my life. Even after getting it and using it, it felt fragile, as if someone could take it away. Sheila and the Warrior Witches were right. I had done nothing wrong. I only exercised my choice with money that I had earned. I knew I had to affirm my own reality over and over again if I didn't want to mistakenly live in someone else's.

It was and is OK to take up space, and I longed for Sanjay to get that. I thought back to an interaction I had with him a few years before when he seemed to understand how challenging I find it to take space for myself.

It was spring, and the sun was shining. I was on my way out the door for a day with my girlfriends. All members of my household were awake, and I could feel their anticipation of what they would do in my absence as these were often "fun" days with Dad. As I was leaving, my husband was focused on tidying up and looked at the basket of my clothes sitting on the family room floor.

I have always struggled to get my laundry folded. Through all the meal prepping, homework helping, mediating, comforting, medicating, running my own business, and so on, folding my laundry has been very low on my list of priorities. Since I'm fortunate enough to have children and a husband who fold their own laundry, my basket is occasionally the only one left on the floor of our family room.

"I have no baskets for my laundry because your clothes have been using them for the past two weeks," Sanjay complained.

I seethed. I was on my way out the door for a "me" day, and I felt extraordinarily resentful that I now needed to respond to this.

Without a word, I stomped into the garage, slamming the door behind me for extra effect. I grabbed one of the cardboard boxes we had just unpacked from our move and brought it inside. I proceeded to stuff all my clean clothes from the laundry basket into this box and marched the box upstairs and threw it into my office. Hands shaking, I came back downstairs, grabbed my bag, paused my emotional state to say goodbye to my children, unpaused, and then stormed out the door.

As I was getting into my car, Sanjay came outside. He walked toward me and stopped.

Crap, now I have to get into it with him.

"You don't have anything sharp in your pockets, do you?" he teased.

I looked at him, wanting him to take this seriously.

"There is no room in this massive house for me!" I exclaimed. "I will never leave my shit around for you to complain about again. I will keep my stuff in my office, and you can have the rest of the house!"

He approached me hesitantly, wrapped his arms around me, and gave me a squeeze.

I rested my head against his chest, surprised at how good it felt.

As I drove away, I realized that my reaction was over the top. I reflected on this idea that within the collective, I often feel as though I am not allowed to exist as an individual. This mindset wasn't something Sanjay had imposed on me, even though we *both* tended to reinforce it due to the culture in which we were both raised. Overcoming this mindset is an ongoing challenge that I continue to work through. I was grateful for my husband's ability to recognize my reaction for what it was and let it go while still maintaining connection.

Even when he was angry or upset, I wanted him to keep the door open for connection or at least leave room for it. It helped me feel more human while processing the feedback I was receiving. I didn't see upgrading my seat as a major issue, and it was OK if Sanjay felt otherwise. All I wanted was to maintain our connection despite our differences so that the cost of taking up space didn't feel so high.

14

Sitayan

Four years ago, I was leading a workshop on self-compassion and personal well-being for women in California when I had one of the most profound realizations of my life. I exhaled deeply as I held a small paperback book in my hands. "Sita was not just Rama's wife, she was a warrioress."

It was 2020, and we were in the middle of the COVID-19 pandemic. Various aspects of life (parenting, work, homeschooling, household responsibilities, and so on) all felt as if they ran together. While I experienced some relief in not having to socialize as much, I longed to connect with like-minded people outside my home. On this day, I was grateful to see friendly faces through my computer screen and be in community with other strong women. I'd been asked by a local psychologist to run a self-love workshop for her weekly group. I stared at the *Brady Bunch* boxes across my screen and felt a swarm of butterflies begin to flutter in my stomach.

The topic for this forty-five-minute session was about learning to trust oneself by challenging external narratives that perhaps we've taken on as our own. I started the session with bits of my own story and the price I had paid for not thinking more critically about the beliefs I was fed. As I spoke, I noticed a South Asian woman in one of the boxes on the screen who had a quiet power about her. I was curious but didn't check in as I was in the middle of my talk. Finally, I had participants go off into breakout rooms to talk to each other about where they might want to challenge things in their own lives. When they returned, the South Asian woman spoke. She asked if she could share a passage from a book and I obliged.

" 'O King of Ayodhya! I address you in this way because you've always placed your role as king ahead of your role as husband . . .'"

Chills ran up my spine. This passage was from *The Forest of Enchantments* by Chitra Bannerjee Divakaruni. The book is a retelling of the Ramayana from Sita's perspective. Sita is the woman, the goddess who has been held as the model of womanhood for Indian girls and women because of her tolerance and devotion to her husband, King Rama.

In this mythological story, Sita is kidnapped by the evil demon Ravana and held captive until her husband comes to rescue her. Before reuniting with Rama, Sita is asked to walk through fire to prove her purity and she complies. When they return to Ayodhya, the city where her husband, King Rama is crowned king, a village washerman begins to spread rumors about Sita's captivity with the demon, alluding to infidelity. At the time of these rumors, Sita was pregnant with twins. Upon hearing these allegations, Rama decides to banish Sita to the forest without telling her in order to appease his countrymen. Now, Sita was standing up.

"Did you stop to think—as a wise king would—that there would always be people who gossip, even in the best-run kingdoms, for it's their nature? Were you compassionate, the way a king is meant to be, when you banished me without telling me what you were about to do, without allowing me to defend myself or choose my destiny? . . ."

I could not believe it. I had never imagined a world in which Sita used her voice in this way.

"And if you were not, shouldn't someone be judging you today?"

"You care so much about the citizens of Ayodhya; did you think of the impact your actions would have on the women of the city? That men would punish their wives harshly or even discard them for the smallest infractions, saying King Rama did so, then why shouldn't I?"

"For the sake of my daughters in the centuries to come, I must now stand up against this unjust action you are asking of me . . . I bless my daughters, who are yet unborn. I pray that if life tests them—as sooner or later life is bound to do—they'll be able to stand steadfast and think carefully, using their hearts as well as their heads, understanding when they need to compromise, and knowing when they must not."

". . . This is one of those times when a woman must stand up and say, No more!"

As she spoke, mother earth cracked open with a roar and engulfed Sita as she returned back to her original home.

I listened and my body shivered, small bumps appearing on my skin. In all the years of reading and listening to the verses and discourse on the Ramayana, never had I heard this. While it was Sita's declaration, it was the missing piece to my own wholeness.

I felt myself apply the very lessons I had just taught as I questioned the role Sita played in this epic story. The role that the men who wrote these stories wanted women to always play.

"Thank you for sharing that passage." I tried to express my gratitude in words, but they did not suffice.

I ordered *The Forest of Enchantments*, and as I read, tears that had been locked up for decades began to fall.

"Rage rises up in me until my whole body is scorched, for some kinds of burning don't require a fire."

Reading these words from Sita, the goddess who embodied the qualities of a "good Indian woman," the one who came down to earth to teach us all how a woman was supposed to live, felt like a calming balm to my heart.

I finished the book on a trip to Oregon, and as I sat by the ocean, I looked out upon it and wept. I cried tears for the voice inside of me that had been too scared to speak up, tears for the doubts I had about being good enough for others, tears for all the South Asian women who decided how they needed to contort themselves in order to be true to their identity.

As I sat there, I felt the ocean holding me as waves of emotion washed over me. I remembered how I was not believed as a young girl of twelve when I told my dad that an older man who was a friend of the family had touched me in ways that didn't feel OK. I remembered Baba's anger when he realized that I told my ex about his abuse and rape. I thought of the shame directed at me from all the onlookers when they saw Baba's frustration, as if I had done something terrible to anger him. I thought of Sanjay and how he blamed me for the abuse and rape I had endured at the hands of that demon. I felt the weight of blame I had silently carried—the blame others had placed on me for the horror I had endured. Reading Sita's words, I felt seen and understood for all the injustice I experienced as a young girl and as a woman. I felt some of my own burden break off and fall away.

It's real. I thought. *I'm not crazy . . .*

***

A year and a half passed, and during that time I often thought of Chitraji's book. I spoke of it often among my Warrior Witch sisters.

One afternoon, as I was getting ready for a girls' weekend with these wonderful women, Mansi texted us. "Chitra Banerjee Divakaruni is in town, and there's a gathering this Sunday evening. Anyone want to go?"

My whole body screamed, "YES!"

This woman is so important to me. She wrote Sita's story as it needed to be written. She wrote it in service of liberating East Indian women, and just through her words, I experienced this freedom.

What would it be like to meet her? Would I be able to convey the impact she's had on me? I really wanted her to know the importance of her book in my life.

After our weekend together, Mansi and I drove to the gathering. I grabbed my copy of *The Forest of Enchantments* and followed my friend in. The yard was lined with beautiful flowers and greenery. There were chairs set up with a large seat at the front which was to be Chitraji's. We found our seats in the front row, and a few minutes later, we heard someone behind us.

"Hello!"

As I looked up, I realized it was Chitraji. I didn't know how to respond. A part of me, accustomed to revering those who have deeply influenced my life, immediately surfaced. But alongside that part was a newer awareness that we are all human, all equal. The tension between these two perspectives created a moment of internal conflict and dissonance.

"Thank you for doing this," I said.

"Would you like me to sign your book?" she asked.

I brought my copy to her.

"This book was life-changing," I told her. "I was raised listening to the Ramayana, and reading your book was so healing for me. I now want to pass it on to my daughter as the version of the story she knows, the Sitayana. Thank you."

"I wanted to create a version of the story that women could feel themselves in. Ram was great, and so was Sita. We don't have to put Ram down to lift Sita up. They were both imperfect beings." I could feel the wisdom radiating out of her as I listened. I had an urge to touch her feet and let her know that I see her as the elder I wish I had in my life, but I resisted, not wanting to make her uncomfortable.

The evening went on, and Chitraji spoke about her work as an author and an advocate for South Asian individuals and families facing domestic violence. I found it inspiring to hear about the organization she and several other women had started for this cause, Maitri*. While there are many groups focused on these issues, I had not heard of anyone else doing this specifically for the South Asian community. It is imperative to understand the cultural aspects of violence within this population in order to provide effective support. It made perfect sense that it was a woman—someone who deeply understood these cultural complexities and nuances—who also chose to give voice to a goddess. Chitraji had created an extraordinary work of art—Sita's story—that offered my heart a new direction in which to seek hope.

This book, and, more specifically, this passage, helped me to reclaim my voice as I linked my cultural identity with my gender. I read Sita's words over and over, and each time, I sensed that the strength, force, and ferocity of this goddess was not only more than I had ever known, but much more than what was taught to me as a child. A deep reverence for Rama had been instilled in me. The Goddess, however, was only introduced as a means to finding a "good husband." I could now sense the immense power she held to defend and advocate for what was right. She was not the embodiment of tolerance as I had been led to believe. I saw her as being fiercely compassionate and compassionately fierce. Her fire was aligned with and often in service of her love. It had been the Goddess who had been rising within me over and over to reclaim myself all these years. This was a Goddess worthy of my worship.

*For more information on this organization, please see the list of resources provided at the end of this book.

15

Reclamation

"Who do you think you are?!" My eyes bulged as I stared at my attacker and screamed in his face.

He slowly backed away, mumbling, *"No one will believe you."* On my hands and knees, I inched forward, intent on making my power known—both to him and to myself. Bringing both hands to the floor, I lay on my side and propelled my leg forward into his face. He fell, and I did it again and again . . .

The instructor blew her whistle and stepped in between me and my assailant.

IMPACT* is a non-profit organization that teaches full force self-defense in a safe and empowering environment. I had heard about it a few years earlier and then again just last year. In May of 2024, I finally found the courage and time to register and take the course. As soon as I did, I messaged the Warrior Witches. "Anyone wanna do this with me?"

All my sisters wanted to; however, it only worked with Reva's schedule. I loved the connection I shared and still share with Reva and was so grateful not to have to do this alone.

Driving to class on the first day, I felt a sense of dread deep in my belly. I had heard about the power of this class, and while that was what prompted me to take this step, I was terrified of what would get stirred up or even what might *not* come up. I wanted to be able to show up differently. I wanted people to be able to feel my presence and boundaries without my having to say anything. I wanted to be one of those people whose boundaries were not in question. Someone who people hesitated to push. *What if that doesn't happen? What if I take the whole course and nothing changes? What if I just don't have that kind of fire within me?*

The class was held in a martial arts dojo. I walked in and was greeted by an incredibly kind woman who showed me what to do before getting settled in on the mat. There were about four other women besides Reva and me attending and four others who seemed to be instructors. I later learned that a large group had just dropped out, and the small size we had in our class was rare. It gave us the opportunity to get to know each other in a slightly deeper way and gave us more time to practice our skills.

We learned several moves that first day and practiced choreographed attacks. I was surprised by the very realistic feel of these fights. One of the instructors wore a heavily padded suit and played the role of aggressor. Each time, this person not only attacked us physically, but used the words an actual assailant would say. They took our blows and sometimes stood back up if we weren't forceful enough. We learned to fight through tears, fear, anger, and many other emotions that show up in the moment when a person is assaulted while also managing the adrenaline that was pumping through our bodies.

On the second day of training, we were asked to come up with a scenario that we would like to practice. It could be a situation that we were afraid of or something that had actually happened in our lives that perhaps we wanted to rewrite. I immediately knew what would be most powerful for me, but I hesitated. If I were to replay the first time that demon assaulted me the day before my first wedding, it could be life changing. I also feared that I might not fight my assailant when the time came, and the exercise might be futile. I thought about how intense it would be and worried about the impact it might have on the rest of the class. I spoke to Reva about it, and she provided the confidence I needed but couldn't access.

When it was time for this activity, I didn't have another scenario in mind, so I went for it. My will to do this was irresolute at best. I described the scenario, and as we began, I left my body. Dissociation is how I managed to get through many things during that time in my life. My body held on to this memory and did what it knew how to do.

I watched as the suited actor came closer. They were playing the part of the demon.

"There you are!" they said affectionately, walking toward me.

Flustered and disoriented, I tried to remember that I was in a role-play. I paused for a moment.

"I'm scared, Babaji."

"It's normal to be afraid before getting married." They put their arm around me.

I did not want to be touched and tried to wiggle my way out from under their arm. Something was off, and while it is completely obvious now, I couldn't place it in the moment.

"Why don't you lie down?" They sat down and motioned for me to do the same.

They said it in the most natural way. It seemed harmless, and for a moment, I was about to oblige. And then, in a split second, I was back in my body.

"No, I'm not going to," I said very slowly, calmly, and softly at first as my body readjusted. I continued to say "No" each time, my voice getting a little louder until I was *ALL* there.

"WHO DO YOU THINK YOU ARE?" I screamed as I lurched forward, my face in their face. "HOW DARE YOU DO THIS?! DO YOU REALLY THINK YOU CAN CONTINUE TO DO THIS? THAT NO ONE WILL KNOW?"

I moved toward them with deliberate, measured steps, almost like a lion stalking its prey, my voice cutting through the air—loud, slow, and unmistakably clear.

"YOU ARE NOTHING MORE THAN A PIECE OF SHIT."

"No one will believe you," they said softly.

"HOW DARE YOU!"

I struck the padded mask they wore on their head with the palm of my hand, and they fell back. I got down to the floor and began kicking their head over and over again as I screamed, "YOU PIECE OF SHIT!"

The instructor stepped between us once my attacker was subdued. Tears poured down my face as adrenaline surged through my body. After this exercise, I sat, my body shaking as I recovered.

I can't believe I was about to lie down! I thought, ashamed.

After class that day, Reva and I hung out at a coffee shop for a while before meeting up with the rest of the Warrior Witches.

"I wondered if you were going to lie down!" Reva told me. "And then, it was like a switch flipped and you beat the shit of out of him! It was so powerful, Chanchal!"

I listened and it hit me. To create new neural pathways around this experience, I had to relive it. That reenactment had taken me back to the days when I was actually with Baba, alone in a room. I was that younger version of me at first, and I had to go through the process of waking up to create change.

I exhaled. Ugh . . . it made sense now. I could be grateful for this experience rather than let it sow even more doubt in myself about whether I would allow someone to take advantage of me even today. I could now trust myself. I could feel the shift I had made but still did not believe it fully.

I've learned that growth happens at a different pace for the body, heart, and mind. My body and heart seem to have made the leap and know how to set effective boundaries. My mind, with only past experiences to go by, does not yet trust in this shift.

I thought back to the trip I made to India last year to meet my Nani's family. It was such a beautiful experience, and I didn't think I would go back for a while. I had done what I needed to do and felt complete. While I felt reconnected with my heritage, I still was not so sure about the culture and wanted to keep my distance. I identified as a member of my lineage; however, I wasn't as comfortable with my identity being Indian.

I was surprised when I was asked to go to India by a retired Stanford professor to help facilitate T-groups at a school for public policy in the South. I felt honored to be asked, and at the same time, terrified of what this experience might be like. I had tried to use the skills from this program with my own family and had failed miserably. *How would people from a culture who have little emotional awareness respond to this sort of training?*

"The founder of the university was an old student of mine and wants to bring the program to his school," the professor told me.

OK, so there is value here. India is such a hierarchical society that if the founder of a large institution deems something important, the rest will fall in line to try to find that value even if they don't see it immediately.

***

It was the first time the other facilitators and I were to meet with the students. We entered a classroom that was similar to the ones I was used to at Stanford. The professor had asked us to demo a T-group at the front of the class for about ten minutes so that the students could get a sense of what it would be like. It was a complicated request, as we needed to show vulnerability toward each other in front of a group we had never met. For me, it felt like an even tougher task because these were all people from my culture, and one of my biggest fears with this group is judgment. My heart pounded, but I decided to go for it, hoping to feel a sense of belonging rather than the distancing criticism I was used to within my community. I sat in the circle with my peers at the front of the room in an awkward silence.

"I'm feeling nervous and excited to be here and do this work. Being born and raised in the US, I've faced questions about my identity even though my ancestry is all Indian. Over the years, I've lost my connection to this country due to painful events, but I am now hoping to reconnect and reclaim my Indian identity on my own terms without anyone telling me how Indian I am or am not based on how I live my life."

That was a lot. I said it, and as I waited for what seemed like hours for a response, I worried about how they would react and whether they would judge me.

"Thank you for sharing all of that, Chanchal," one of my peers responded. "I could feel how tender that was for you, and I'm imagining how powerful it must be to be here in the country of your ancestors."

I exhaled, grateful for the acknowledgement of the complexity of my situation. I also realized that this was my reclamation of my Indianness. I was here among my cultural peers, about to share and listen deeply. We were going to get beyond the surface-level talk and beyond communication that was contingent upon "*Log kya kehenge?*" (What will other people say?) The idea excited me even though I wasn't quite sure yet if we would be able to do it.

By the second day of the four-day T-group weekend, we had found our rhythm. Members of our group had shared deeply personal experiences and were met with compassion and empathy. When I opened up about my own story, I was greeted with an outpouring of affection and, to my surprise, respect. What astonished me most was hearing the men in our group speak openly about the patriarchy as something that needed to be challenged and dismantled.

In this space, I felt myself healing and reclaiming parts of my identity. It was deeply comforting to be Indian among others who not only honored fundamental human values but were also willing to acknowledge where those values were being overlooked. These students represented the next generation of India—a generation that clearly loves its culture, country, and heritage, while also recognizing the urgent need for change in certain areas.

Ancient wisdom is beautiful and imperfect. The ability to discern what to build on and learn from versus what needs to be cast aside has been a huge part of my journey. I now realize that the beliefs I hold at any moment are not all mine. Some have been passed down to me, while others have been absorbed from the society and community in which I live. These beliefs can often blend seamlessly into my daily life, making them difficult to recognize. Uncovering them takes intention and examining them to see if they still hold true for me is an even greater challenge.

I've learned that whenever a belief is rigid, hierarchical, or treated as an unquestionable truth, it has likely lost its vitality—its ability to grow, evolve, and stay relevant. These kinds of beliefs have often led me to seek answers outside myself, only to find that what I was searching for could never be found there. True wisdom, I've realized, is not fixed—it lives and breathes through continuous inquiry within. This is where I found self-awareness, self-compassion, and my own power.

Now, as I look back on my life so far, I am grateful for all of it. I continue to learn and grow as I reclaim myself and my agency. My experiences have created the bedrock of who I am today. They have opened my heart in some ways and created boundaries in others. The more I stand in my sovereignty—choosing to believe in it and live by it—the more those around me can feel its presence and either honor it or walk away. In this way, my soul naturally shapes my relationships, drawing in those who can meet me in true connection.

My healing journey has involved balancing bold self-expression with the vulnerability needed to accept the right support. For years, I struggled in therapy until I recognized the need for a culturally aware therapist. Understanding that my family's norms differ from mainstream American society, I found that a therapist who appreciated these cultural nuances could provide the unbiased support necessary for effective healing.

When working with therapists who lacked this cultural awareness, I struggled to be genuinely vulnerable, despite playing the role of a "good client." It wasn't until I found a therapist who understood my cultural background that I could finally lower my defenses and engage authentically in the therapeutic process.

***

Sanjay and I continue to work on truly seeing and adoring each other in all our pain and glory. Coming from a collectivist culture that traditionally assigns power to men, we are both committed to recognizing and addressing our internalized patterns and biases. This effort allows us to better support our individual and mutual healing, as we strive for both personal and shared autonomy.

Reflecting on the thirty-six years since I first encountered my abuser, I hardly recognize the person I was back then. I realize that this journey of self-discovery feels endless, as my soul is slowly revealing its true essence to me over a lifetime.

Writing this book has been both an arduous and a healing journey. Each word on these pages represents a step toward reclaiming my power—a journey through the depths of trauma and pain, and a rise into self-awareness and strength. While my story is undeniably marked by moments of profound suffering, these experiences have served as the crucible that forged my resilience, wisdom, and inner strength. They compelled me to stop seeking validation and power from the outside world and instead recognize the immense divinity and power that has always resided within me. This is a process I continue to work on today.

In many ways, the process of writing became a mirror, reflecting back the lessons learned and the growth achieved along the way. It demanded that I confront the parts of myself I once feared or denied. Yet through this confrontation, I discovered a profound sense of gratitude for every challenge I've faced. The reflection made clear that true power and healing are not found in external sources but rather arise from within—through embracing our full selves, both our light and our shadows.

Today, I have the profound privilege of guiding women on their journeys of self-discovery, helping them to uncover and embrace their innate magic, power, and divinity. I am witness to their remarkable transformations as they find the courage to voice their long-held desires, frustrations, and fears, finally being heard in ways they never imagined possible. I am honored to sit in circles with fierce, empowered women—goddesses who are here to make a difference in the world. Watching them uplift and inspire one another to step into their full potential is truly awe-inspiring.

As I close this chapter, I do so with a deep sense of peace and empowerment, knowing that my story, in all its rawness and truth, might inspire others to embark on their own journeys of self-discovery and healing. May this book serve as a reminder that within each of us lies the power to transform our pain into purpose and our suffering into strength, and ultimately to find the divinity that resides within.

*For more information on this organization, please see the list of resources provided at the end of this book.

Notes on Language and Culture

Aarti
A Hindu religious ritual of worship in which light from wicks soaked in ghee (purified butter) or camphor are offered to one or more deities. This ritual is typically performed at the end of worship.

Akhyana
A traditional storytelling method often used in Indian religious or cultural settings.

Alu Matar Sabzi
A popular North Indian dish made with potatoes (alu) and green peas (matar) in a spiced tomato gravy.

Bhabhi
Sister-in-law, specifically the wife of one's brother.

Bhai Sahib
A respectful term for addressing an elder brother or a respected male figure.

Beta
An affectionate term meaning "child" or "son" in Hindi and other Indian languages.

Bindis
Decorative dots worn on the forehead, traditionally by women, often symbolizing marriage or spirituality.

Bua
Paternal aunt; father's sister.

Chacha
Paternal uncle; father's younger brother.

Chachi
The wife of one's paternal uncle (Chacha).

Chopai
A quatrain or verse, often from Hindu scripture or poetry.

Dahl
Lentils, which are a staple in Indian cuisine.

Devanagari
The script used for writing Sanskrit, Hindi, and several other Indian languages.

Govardhan
A sacred hill in Vrindavan, associated with the deity Krishna.

Har ki Paudi
A famous ghat (steps leading to a river) in Haridwar, India, known for its religious significance on the banks of the Ganges River. Literal translation: Steps to God.

Harmonium
A keyboard instrument similar to a small organ, often used in Indian devotional music.

Havan Kund
A fire pit used in Hindu rituals for offerings and prayers.

'Ji'
An honorific suffix or title used in Hindi and other Indian languages.

Kali-Ma

A Hindu goddess, often associated with empowerment, destruction, and transformation.

Kanyadhan

A Hindu wedding ritual where the bride's parents (primarily her father) give her away to the groom as a gift or donation (a "selfless act") and relinquish their responsibilities toward their daughter, placing her care and future in the hands of her husband.

Karva Chauth

A traditional Hindu festival celebrated primarily in North India by married women. Observed on the fourth day after the full moon in the Hindu month of Kartika (October–November), it is a day-long fast during which women pray for the long life, health, and prosperity of their husbands.

Kirtan

A form of devotional singing or chanting, often accompanied by musical instruments.

Krishna

A major deity in Hinduism, revered as the eighth avatar of Vishnu and celebrated for his love, compassion, and divine playfulness. Known for his many consorts, Krishna with Radha Rani symbolizes divine love. Krishna's teachings in the *Bhagavad Gita* and his playful exploits in the *Bhagavata Purana* are central to Hindu devotion.

KumKum

A red powder used for religious and cultural markings, such as on the forehead.

Lehngas
Traditional Indian skirts often worn by women during special occasions or festivals.

Mama
Maternal uncle; mother's brother.

Mandap
A decorated structure or canopy under which Hindu wedding rituals are performed.

Masi
Maternal aunt; mother's sister.

Mausa
The husband of one's maternal aunt (Masi).

Mehndi
Henna, often applied to hands and feet during weddings and festivals.

Nana
Maternal grandfather.

Pandit
A Hindu priest or scholar, especially one well-versed in scriptures and rituals.

Parandi
A traditional decorative hair accessory used in braids, often in Punjabi culture.

Puja
A Hindu worship ritual involving offerings to deities.

Puri
Deep-fried Indian bread made from unleavened dough.

Radha Rani
A revered figure in Hinduism, often seen as the consort of Krishna and the embodiment of devotion.

Radhe
A term used in devotion to Radha, often paired with Krishna in chants.

Raksha Bandhan
A festival celebrating the bond between brothers and sisters, symbolized by tying a Rakhi (sacred thread).

Rakhi
A thread tied by a sister on her brother's wrist during Raksha Bandhan as a symbol of protection and love.

Ramayana
An ancient Indian epic that narrates the life and adventures of Lord Rama.

Roti
Unleavened flatbread, a staple in Indian cuisine.

Sabzi
Vegetable dishes, often cooked with spices.

Salwaar Kameez
A traditional outfit consisting of a tunic (kameez) and pants (salwaar), often worn by women in South Asia.

Saas
Mother-in-law.

Sari

A traditional garment worn by women in South Asia, consisting of a long piece of fabric draped around the body.

Sitayana

A retelling of the Ramayana from Sita's (Rama's wife) perspective.

Tablas

A pair of hand-played drums used in Indian classical and devotional music.

Talis

A term often used for sacred or decorative plates.

A Guided Dialogue from My Story to Yours

These questions are designed for you to reflect on the themes from this book as they relate to your own life. Some may stir something tender, others may affirm what you already know. They're not meant to lead you anywhere specific, but to support you in reclaiming your story—on your terms, in your time.

Use what resonates. Leave what doesn't.

You might choose journal privately, meditate on your reflections, share them with a trusted friend, or use them in a book club setting. If you're facilitating a group discussion, selecting 1–3 questions per chapter can be a supportive way to keep conversation grounded and spacious.

These aren't questions you answer once and move on from—they're living questions. Ones you can return to again and again. Your responses may shift as you grow, heal, and uncover new layers of yourself. The most important thing is to honor whatever truth is present for you in this moment—exactly as you are, wherever you are in your journey.

Chapter 1: Ramayana

1. What aspects of your identity feel deeply authentic to who you are? Are there parts of your identity that you've embraced to feel a sense of belonging? How do these elements shape your understanding of yourself?

2. In what ways have you shaped your actions or choices to meet the expectations of your parents, caregivers, or significant others? How do these actions align with your personal values and aspirations?

3. Are there identities or communities you find yourself navigating between? What opportunities and challenges arise from being part of multiple identities, and how do you honor the complexity of your experience?

4. How do you define the difference between fitting in and truly belonging? Reflect on moments in your life when you've experienced each—what did you notice about how you felt, and what does that reveal about your needs and values?

Chapter 2: The Stage

1. When have you expressed yourself in a way that felt authentic to you, even if it challenged norms or expectations? What did you learn from that experience about your values or courage? If this feels unfamiliar, what might it look like for you to take that kind of step in the future?

2. Reflect on a time when you shared something deeply meaningful to you. How did others respond, and how did that experience shape your views on vulnerability or connection?

3. Have you ever felt limited by others' assumptions about who you are or what you can do? How did you navigate that

experience, and what insights did it give you about yourself or others?

4. Think of a time when you faced an opportunity or challenge that felt overwhelming or beyond your readiness. How did you respond, and what did you learn about your capacity to grow or seek support?

5. What does belonging mean to you, and how is it different from simply fitting in? Reflect on a time you felt a strong sense of belonging—what made that experience meaningful?

Chapter 3: Infatuation

1. Think of a time when you felt deeply inspired by someone or something. What drew you in, and how did that relationship or experience shape your sense of purpose or values?

2. How do you navigate situations where someone you admire is questioned or criticized by others? What helps you decide whether to hold on to your beliefs or reconsider them?

3. Reflect on a time when someone changed your perspective on something or someone you once strongly believed in. What made you open to that change, and how did it affect your relationships or worldview?

4. What qualities do you look for in a teacher, mentor, or leader? How do you decide whom to trust and learn from, especially when there are conflicting opinions about their character?

Chapter 4: Infatuation

1. Think of a time when you felt deeply committed to a person, idea, or cause. What sacrifices did you make for that commitment, and how did those choices affect your life?

2. Have you ever been so focused on someone or something that it overshadowed other important parts of your life? How did you recognize this imbalance, and what did you learn from the experience?

3. Who or what has had a significant influence on your decisions or actions? How do you distinguish between healthy inspiration and a level of influence that might not serve your well-being?

4. Have you ever pushed yourself beyond your physical, emotional, or mental limits in pursuit of something you cared about? Looking back, how did that experience shape your understanding of self-care and boundaries?

Chapter 5: The Dream

1. Reflect on times when you've silenced your own voice to maintain harmony or avoid conflict. What inner truths have you ignored in these moments, and what would it look like to honor them instead?

2. What are some ways you protect yourself from pain or discomfort, such as justifying someone's harmful behavior or suppressing challenging emotions? How might these patterns keep you safe but also limit your authenticity or growth?

3. Have you ever experienced a stark contrast in someone's behavior or how they treat you, leaving you feeling confused

or uncertain? How do you navigate these contradictions, and what helps you trust your own perceptions?

4. Reflect on moments when you've felt "not enough" to challenge harmful behaviors or situations. What messages or beliefs might be holding you back, and how can you cultivate the courage to act differently?

5. Do you ever find yourself pretending there is closeness or intimacy in a relationship where it doesn't truly exist? How do you discern between real connection and superficial bonds, and what steps can you take to seek more authentic relationships?

Chapter 6: The Good Girl

1. Have you ever felt that your identity became reduced to a single role or expectation, such as being a partner, caregiver, or professional? How did that affect your sense of self, and what steps can you take to reclaim parts of your identity that feel authentic?

2. Have you ever felt pressured to give up aspects of your independence or past life to maintain a relationship? How did that experience shape your understanding of compromise versus self-sacrifice, and what would healthy balance look like for you?

3. After experiencing a major life change, such as leaving a relationship, role, or environment, how do you navigate feelings of emptiness or loss? What helps you rediscover your sense of purpose and redefine yourself on your own terms?

4. Have you ever faced a decision where leaving a harmful situation felt as dangerous or uncertain as staying? What gave you the courage to act, and how do you reflect on that choice now?

5. Reflect on any labels or identities you've carried—such as being divorced, single, or otherwise outside societal norms—that made you feel conflicted or judged. How do you move toward embracing these parts of your story as sources of strength rather than shame?

6. Have you ever been in a situation where trusting someone else's choices or actions put you at risk, as with the seatbelt incident? How do you balance trust in others with advocating for your safety and well-being?

7. Reflect on how you navigate control in your relationships. Are there areas where you try to exert control, or where you feel controlled by others? How does this dynamic affect your well-being and the health of your relationships?

8. Are there areas in your life where you are holding back from taking action that could significantly improve your circumstances? What fears or concerns might be stopping you, and what steps could you take to move forward?

Chapter 7: Wounded

1. Reflect on a time when you felt responsible for something outside of your control, like someone else's actions or decisions. How can you reframe these experiences to offer yourself compassion rather than blame?

2. Have you ever trusted someone and felt let down, as with lending money or seeking guidance? How can you use those

experiences to better define boundaries while still maintaining openness in relationships?

3. How do you navigate the balance between supporting loved ones and prioritizing your own needs? Are there moments when you've felt stretched too thin, and how did you handle them?

4. Have you ever hesitated to ask for help because you feared it might make you appear weak or incapable? How might reaching out for support actually reflect strength and resilience?

5. How do you define being self-sufficient? In what ways do you feel confident in taking care of yourself, and where might you need support or growth?

6. Reflect on times when you felt like a failure, whether financially, emotionally, or otherwise. How might you redefine success in a way that honors your efforts, growth, and ability to persevere through difficult circumstances?

Chapter 8: From Dating to Yoga

1. In your relationships, how do you balance supporting a partner's needs with advocating for your own? Reflect on a time when this balance felt off—what did you learn, and what steps might help you create healthier dynamics moving forward?

2. Have you ever pursued a goal or dream (like opening a business or switching careers) while juggling other significant life responsibilities? How do you define success for yourself, and what does fulfillment look like in your personal and professional life?

3. Reflect on a moment when family questions, comments, or judgments affected your sense of self. How have these interactions shaped your relationships with your family, and what steps might help you set healthy boundaries or heal old wounds?

4. Life transitions—such as marriage, career changes, or parenthood—often bring unexpected challenges and growth. How have you adapted to major transitions in your life, and what strategies have helped you stay grounded while evolving into new roles?

Chapter 9: Waking Up

1. Reflect on a time when you realized something profound about a relationship, belief, or community you were deeply attached to. How did you navigate the doubt or resistance that arose, and what helped you stay true to your realization?

2. Have you ever been in a situation where you had to trust your intuition over the advice or opinions of others? What did you learn about yourself from that experience, and how can you continue to strengthen your trust in your own judgment?

3. Reflect on a time when you had to let go of a person, belief, or community that no longer aligned with who you were becoming. How did this process affect your sense of identity, and what helped you move forward?

4. When faced with challenges that others couldn't fully understand—whether related to health, family, or personal growth—what helped you find the strength to advocate for yourself or your loved ones? How can you build on that strength in other areas of your life?

5. Think about a life-changing experience, such as becoming a parent, starting a new practice, or navigating a major transition. How did this experience empower you to trust yourself more deeply, and how has it influenced the way you make decisions?

Chapter 10: Falling Apart

1. Have you ever experienced a time when you were dealing with emotional pain or trauma and felt unsupported by those around you? How did you cope, and what would have helped you feel more understood or cared for?

2. Anger can feel overwhelming when there's no outlet for it. How do you process and release anger in healthy ways, especially when it stems from feeling unheard or dismissed? What could help you create a safe space for this?

3. Reflect on a situation where someone offered forgiveness but used it to maintain control or silence you. How did that dynamic affect your ability to express yourself, and how might you approach such situations differently in the future?

4. Have you ever felt that your voice or needs were minimized in a relationship? How did you recognize this, and what steps did you take—or could you take—to advocate for mutual respect and understanding?

5. Reflect on a time when you realized a relationship or dynamic was no longer healthy for you. What signs made this clear, and how did you find the courage to make a change or set boundaries?

Chapter 11: Training

1. Reflect on a time when something you once loved lost its meaning or joy because you felt pressured to meet external expectations. How did you recognize this, and what steps did you take—or could you take—to realign with what feels authentic to you?

2. Have you ever pursued a personal or professional goal despite doubts or questions from others, such as concerns about its practicality or return on investment? How did you stay motivated, and what did you learn about trusting your own vision?

3. Reflect on a time when you felt truly heard and validated by others. How did that experience shape your understanding of the importance of being present for others? In what ways can you create space for both receiving and offering this kind of support?

4. What role does community play in your growth and healing? How do you identify or build relationships with people who genuinely support and uplift you?

5. Reflect on a time when you decided to pivot from one path to another, whether professionally, personally, or creatively. What inspired the change, and how did embracing a new direction shape your understanding of your values and purpose?

Chapter 12: My Name Set Me Free

1. Reflect on the significance of your name. Does it carry a connection to your history, culture, or personal identity? If you could choose a name for yourself, what would it represent, and why?

2. Have you ever felt the need to redefine or reclaim part of your identity—whether through a name, role, or other aspect of yourself? What inspired this change, and how did you navigate the reactions of others?

3. Is there someone in your family or ancestry you feel a deep connection to, even if you never met them? What does their story or legacy mean to you, and how does it shape your understanding of who you are?

4. Reflect on a time when you struggled to let go of control or fully surrender to a process, whether it was a personal journey, a decision, or a relationship. What did you learn about trust, both in yourself and in the unknown?

5. Think about a time when you made a decision that felt deeply personal or transformative, but others in your life resisted it. How did you stay committed to your choice, and what did you learn about standing firm in your truth?

Chapter 13: Motherland

1. Reflect on a time when you reconnected with your roots, family history, or a place that holds meaning for you. What did this experience teach you about yourself, and how did it shape your understanding of where you come from?

2. Reflect on a time when you had the privilege or opportunity to speak up for someone with less power or voice. How did you use that privilege, and what did you learn about the impact of your actions?

3. Think of a time when you doubted a choice you made, even though it felt right to you. How did you work through that doubt, and what helped you trust your judgment in the end?

4. Reflect on a time when someone close to you understood a personal struggle you faced. How did that understanding strengthen your relationship, and how can you foster similar understanding in your current relationships?

Chapter 14: Sitayan

1. Reflect on a time when you discovered a new perspective or insight that felt like a missing piece of your personal story. How did this new understanding affect the way you see yourself or your past?

2. Are there stories, cultural beliefs, or traditions you've been raised with that feel incomplete or one-sided? How might exploring different perspectives within these stories deepen your understanding of yourself or your heritage?

3. Think of a time when you admired someone deeply. How did you navigate the balance between respecting them and maintaining healthy boundaries to avoid idealization? What did this teach you about relationships?

4. Reflect on a moment when you or someone you admired stood up to injustice, even within a relationship or community. How did this act of courage inspire or influence you, and how might you bring that energy into your own life?

Chapter 15: Reclamation

1. Reflect on a moment in your life where you wish you could have responded differently. How might imagining an alternative response, where you act with strength or clarity, help you reclaim power in your own story?

2. Have you experienced moments where you doubted yourself due to past mistakes? What steps have you taken—or could you take—to trust your growth and focus on your progress rather than your setbacks?

3. Reflect on how you navigate the balance between loving your culture or community and recognizing where change is needed. How do you approach advocating for progress while honoring what you cherish?

The Unearthed Way

The Unearthed Way offers a range of transformative services inspired by Chanchal's journey, as detailed in her book. These offerings empower women leaders to step into their full identity and power through immersive retreats, online programs, personalized sessions, and executive leadership coaching. By focusing on self-awareness, authentic leadership, and relationship navigation, The Unearthed Way provides practical and actionable pathways for personal and professional growth.

Books to Support your Journey

Beattie, Melody. *The New Codependency: Help and Guidance for Today's Generation*
Navigate the complexities of codependency to reclaim your independence and sense of self-worth.

Bradford, David and Carole Robin. *Connect: Building Exceptional Relationships with Family, Friends, and Colleagues*
Enhance your relationships and sense of self through the power of authentic communication and connection.

Divakaruni, Chitra Banerjee. *The Forest of Enchantments*
Experience the retelling of a classic epic through the lens of a powerful female protagonist, exploring themes of identity and resilience.

Divakaruni, Chitra Banerjee. *The Palace of Illusions*
Revisit an ancient tale through the eyes of a woman who redefines her destiny and asserts her identity amid a patriarchal world.

Doyle, Glennon. *Untamed*
Uncover the liberating journey of breaking free from societal limitations to live a life true to your own desires and identity.

Dunlap, Tori. *Financial Feminist: Overcome the Patriarchy's Bullsh*t to Master Your Money and Build a Life You Love*
Empower yourself with financial literacy and independence, breaking free from traditional constraints to claim your financial identity.

Estés, Clarissa Pinkola. *Women Who Run with the Wolves: Myths and Stories of the Wild Woman Archetype*
Delve into the myths and stories that reveal the wild, instinctual nature of women, empowering them to reclaim their true selves.

Foo, Stephanie. *What My Bones Know: A Memoir of Healing from Complex Trauma*
Journey through trauma and healing to rediscover your identity and inner strength.

Gupta, Prachi. *They Called Us Exceptional and Other Lies That Raised Us*
Unpack the complexities of cultural identity and familial expectations in the pursuit of self-discovery and empowerment.

Hersey, Tricia. *Rest Is Resistance: Free yourself*
Embrace rest as a radical act of self-care and resistance, reclaiming your power and identity in a demanding world.

Johnson, Kimberly Ann. *Call of the Wild: How We Heal Trauma, Awaken Our Own Power, and Use It for Good*
Reconnect with your primal instincts and feminine power to reclaim your authentic self.

Kaur, Neelu. **Be Your Own Cheerleader:** *An Asian and South Asian Woman's Cultural, Psychological, and Spiritual Guide to Self-Promote at Work*
Cultivate self-empowerment and confidence to navigate personal and professional challenges with authenticity.

Kohli, Sahaj Kaur. *But What Will People Say? Navigating Mental Health, Identity, Love, and Family Between Cultures*
Explore the journey of navigating cultural expectations and societal pressures to embrace your authentic self.

Lang, Maya. *What We Carry: A Memoir*
Reflect on the intergenerational stories and burdens we inherit and how they shape our sense of self and identity.

Neff, Kristen. *Fierce Self-Compassion: How Women Can Harness Kindness to Speak Up, Claim Their Power, and Thrive*
Discover the transformative power of self-compassion as a tool for reclaiming your identity and harnessing inner strength.

Rawlinson, Jas. *The Stories We Carry*
Explore the narratives that shape our identities and learn how to transform them into sources of empowerment.

Schwartz, Richard C. *No Bad Parts: Healing Trauma and Restoring Wholeness with the Internal Family Systems Model*
Embrace all aspects of yourself with compassion and understanding, transforming internal conflicts into sources of strength.

Taylor, Sonya Renee. *The Body Is Not an Apology: The Power of Radical Self-Love*
Challenge societal norms and embrace radical self-love as a means to reclaim your body and identity.

Urbaniak, Kasia. *Unbound: A Woman's Guide to Power*
Learn how to reclaim your voice and power in a world that often seeks to silence women, through practical strategies and insights.

Culturally Aware Therapists

Asiansformentalhealth.com

Helloalma.com

Inclusivetherapists.com

National Queer & Trans Therapists of Color Network: nqttcn.com

Southasiantherapists.org

Therapyforblackgirls.com

Organizations that Offer Support for Women in Abusive Situations
Helplines in India

Women Helpline (1091)

National Commission for Women (NCW) Helpline: 7827170170

Access to local legal or psychological services.

Impact
www.impactselfdefense.org

Offers comprehensive violence prevention programs such as personal safety, assertiveness, and full force self-defense training.

International Federation of Women Lawyers (FIDA)
https://www.fidafederation.org/

Works globally to provide legal aid for women.

Love Is Respect (US)
Helpline: 1-866-331-9474

Focuses on teen dating and young adult relationships but has solid resources on emotional abuse and setting boundaries.

Maitri
www.maitri.org

A free, confidential, nonprofit organization based in the San Francisco Bay Area that primarily helps families and individuals from South Asia (Afghanistan, Bangladesh, Bhutan, India, Nepal, Pakistan, Sri Lanka, and the Maldives) facing domestic violence, emotional abuse, cultural alienation, or family conflict.

Narika (US-based)
narika.org

Provides free helplines, support groups, and outreach programs for South Asian women facing domestic violence.

The National Domestic Violence Hotline (US)
1-800-799-SAFE (7233) or thehotline.org

Offers 24/7 confidential support, resources, and referrals for those facing domestic violence.

RAINN (Rape, Abuse & Incest National Network)
1-800-656-HOPE (4673) or rainn.org

The largest anti-sexual-violence organization in the US.

Sakhi
sakhi.org

An organization that offers services to survivors of gender-based violence. Sakhi's mission is to promote the safety, stability, and happiness of survivors.

SNEHA (India)
snehamumbai.org

An organization in India supporting women through crisis counseling, healthcare, and violence prevention.

Women for Women International
womenforwomen.org

Works in conflict-ridden regions to support women's empowerment and rights.

About the Author

 Chanchal Garg is a speaker, author, executive coach, and conscious leadership facilitator. She transforms lives by helping clients break through limiting beliefs and build authentic, liberatory connections. Drawing on her MBA and her lived experiences, she addresses difficult truths directly while fostering environments of openness and collaboration.

For over eight years, Chanchal has facilitated Stanford University's Graduate School of Business's most popular elective course on interpersonal dynamics, impacting over 500 future business leaders. She is also the founder of Real Space, a thriving coaching practice, where she guides leaders to transcend cultural and societal constraints, harnessing their personal power in both work and life.

Chanchal wrote *Unearthed: The Lies We Carry and the Truths They Bury* as a deeply personal reclamation—and as an offering. Her voice has been featured at events like Lululemon's International Women's Day gathering and on podcasts such as *She Has the Mic* and *I Don't Give a Should*.

Those Who Held Me . . .

There are so many people who supported me as I wrote this book, and each left an imprint on its pages in his or her own way. Some walked beside me through my darkest moments; others lifted me up when I doubted myself; and many offered wisdom, love, or simply a space to be seen. While I cannot name everyone here, please know that I am deeply grateful for each and every person who has touched this journey. Your presence—whether brief or enduring—has mattered.

Sanj, thank you for being exactly who you are, and for the ways in which our journey has shaped me, revealing truths I needed to see. In your own way, you helped me find clarity, and, in time, a path that felt more aligned. Thank you for the love that has made space for something beautiful to emerge.

Arjun, my thoughtful, kind, and deeply loving son, you are my constant reminder that unconditional love is real, that it exists in its purest form, and that I am deserving of it. Thank you for showing me a love that is boundless.

Sia, my brave, fearless, and courageous warrior—you woke me up. Your existence has been my revolution and my greatest awakening. Thank you for choosing me as your mother and for teaching me every day what it means to stand in my truth.

Warrior Witch Sisters, my unwavering circle of strength and love—you have been my anchors, my mirrors, and my fiercest supporters. Your presence has been a sanctuary where I could speak my truth, be challenged, be validated, and be held without question.

You reminded me, time and time again, that I am capable, worthy, and powerful, even when I struggled to see it for myself.

Mansi—thank you for doing your own ancestral work and letting me witness the truth of your inner world along the way. For being the voice of reason—not performatively, not for show—but with grounded clarity and a steady kind of badassery that calls everyone higher.

Reva, for always showing up to listen, reflect, and name what I sometimes couldn't yet see. For your gentle, piercing truths, and for getting lost in parking lots with me. Thank you for your companionship in both disorientation and clarity.

Sheila, for the work you do in the world and the care you bring to your own motherhood. When you called me after reading my manuscript, you gave me something I didn't know I needed. Your words made this book feel real. You told me you were proud of me—and it landed in a way I'll never forget.

Thank you all for standing by me—always in favor of my growth, always lighting the way toward my own evolution.

Safoura, thank you for seeing me in ways that few ever have. For holding me, walking with me, and patiently supporting me as I rebuilt my trust—not just in life, but in people. Your presence was a gift when I needed it most, and I cherish it deeply.

Reena, thank you for your bold honesty and for seeing me when I was still learning to see myself. You had the courage to tell me the truth about my life, even when it was hard to hear. Your belief in the life I deserved helped me believe in it, too. Thank you for your unwavering faith in me.

Lena, no matter the distance, no matter the time, you've always been there. Even when life pulled us in different directions, I never doubted for a moment that you had my back. You taught me what true loyalty looks like, and for that, I love you.

Jas Rawlinson, your guidance, encouragement, and unshakable belief in my ability to tell this story made all the difference. There were moments when I wasn't sure I could make it through this process, but you never wavered. Your faith in me carried me forward, and for that, I am forever grateful.

Mom, thank you for giving me hope when I had none. Your words—"if it isn't according to your nature, it has to change"— became my lifeline, my guiding light. I carry them with me, always, as a reminder that I have the power to transform my own life. Thank you for giving me that gift.

Dad, thank you for loving me in the way you knew how. Our love has had its own language and its own complexities, and I know it has always been there. For that, I am grateful.

Mausa, thank you for stepping in when I couldn't step up for myself. Your unwavering presence, your belief in my choices, and your willingness to stand beside me gave me the strength to choose my own path. Thank you for showing me that I am never alone.

Shami Mama, thank you for your quiet strength. There were moments that were dark, terrifying, and impossible to navigate alone, and yet, you stood as a shield, protecting me in ways I will never forget. Thank you for your courage and for the safety you gave me in moments when I needed it most.

Alexis Douglas, thank you for seeing my power even before I did. You held up a mirror to my potential, refusing to let me shrink from it. Your leadership, your unwavering support, and your ability to remind me of my own strength have been invaluable. Thank you for always calling me into my greatness.

Chitra Banerjee Divakaruni, your writing was a portal into a powerful feminine heritage I had always longed to connect with. Through your words, I saw myself, my lineage, and the untamed, sacred power that has always existed within me. Thank you for that gift.

My book club ladies, who walked beside me through this journey of completing my book, thank you. Your enthusiasm, your encouragement, and your ability to lift me up when I needed it most helped me hold on to my own excitement. Writing is often a lonely process, but you made sure I never felt alone.

Tiffany Neuman, thank you for helping me shape my story not just on the page, but in the world. Your brilliance in branding, your ability to reflect my voice back to me, and your unwavering belief in my power reminded me, again and again, of who I am. Thank you for seeing my light and helping me shine it even brighter.

Kathryn Velasco, thank you for your steady hand, sharp eye, and fierce commitment to truth. You gently but firmly invited me to stop circling the hard things and meet them head-on. In doing so, you helped me tell a more honest story—not just for the page, but for myself. Your questions pushed me to reflect more deeply, write more clearly, and ultimately, create a book that can truly meet the hearts of its readers.

Nanda, thank you for reminding me that this book is, above all, mine—to shape, to own, to bring into the world on my terms. In a process that often felt overwhelming, you cut through the noise and showed me that publishing doesn't have to be as complicated as it's made out to be. Your encouragement pushed me to take full responsibility for every piece of this journey, and in doing so, once again, I found not just my voice, but a deeper trust in myself. I am grateful.

To every person who has played a role in this journey—whether through a kind word, a moment of encouragement, or simply by believing in me when I couldn't believe in myself—thank you. This book exists because of the love, strength, and support I have received from so many. I carry your presence, your lessons, and your love with me, always.

The Unearthed Way

A Leadership Path for Women Who Refuse to Lead Halfway

The Unearthed Way is for women leaders who are done with shrinking, code-switching, and walking the tightrope of conflicting expectations. It's for those who want to lead with clarity and power—without hardening, without apology, and without losing themselves.

This framework is built on deep self-awareness, relational intelligence, and embodied leadership—giving you the tools to navigate complexity, hold your ground, and expand your leadership range while staying deeply connected to who you are.

Through immersive experiences, cohort-based learning, and personalized coaching, The Unearthed Way offers multiple pathways for growth.